305.50944
MOR

D1339784

STUDIES IN ECONOMIC AND SOCIAL HISTORY

This series, specially commissioned by the Economic History Society, provides a guide to the current interpretations of the key themes of economic and social history in which advances have recently been made or in which there has been significant debate.

Originally entitled 'Studies in Economic History', in 1974 the series had its scope extended to include topics in social history, and the new series title, 'Studies in Economic and Social History', signalises this development.

The series gives readers access to the best work done, helps them to draw their own conclusions in major fields of study, and by means of the critical bibliography in each book guides them in the selection of further reading. The aim is to provide a springboard to further work rather than a set of pre-packaged conclusions or short-cuts.

ECONOMIC HISTORY SOCIETY

The Economic History Society, which numbers over 3000 members, publishes the *Economic History Review* four times a year (free to members) and holds an annual conference. Enquiries about membership should be addressed to the Assistant Secretary, Economic History Society, Peterhouse, Cambridge. Full-time students may join at special rates.

D

136184

STUDIES IN ECONOMIC AND SOCIAL HISTORY

Edited for the Economic History Society by T.C. Smout

PUBLISHED

OTHER TITLES ARE IN PREPARATION

Class and Class Consciousness in the Industrial Revolution 1780—1850

Prepared for
The Economic History Society by

R. J. MORRIS
Lecturer in Economic History,
University of Edinburgh

**HILLCROFT COLLEGE
LIBRARY**
SOUTH BANK
SURBITON
SURREY KT6 6DF

© The Economic History Society 1979

All rights reserved. No part of this publication
may be reproduced or transmitted, in any form
or by any means, without permission.

First edition 1979
Reprinted 1979, 1982, 1983
Published by
THE MACMILLAN PRESS LTD
London and Basingstoke
Companies and representatives
throughout the world

ISBN 0 333 15454 1

Printed and bound in Hong Kong

Contents

Acknowledgements

I should like to thank the following for encouragement, comments and advice: Geoffrey Crossick, Michael Flinn, Barbara Morris, Christopher Smout, Rick Trainor and Margaret Williamson.

R. J. M.

Note on References

References in the text within square brackets relate to the items listed alphabetically in sections I and II of the Select Bibliography, followed, where necessary, by the page numbers in italics; for example [R. Williams, 1958: *13*]. Other references in the text, numbered consecutively throughout the book, relate to the Notes and References section.

Editor's Preface

SINCE 1968, when the Economic History Society and Macmillan published the first of the 'Studies in Economic and Social History', the series has established itself as a major teaching tool in universities, colleges and schools, and as a familiar landmark in serious bookshops throughout the country. A great deal of the credit for this must go to the wise leadership of its first editor, Professor M. W. Flinn, who retired at the end of 1977. The books tend to be bigger now than they were originally, and inevitably more expensive; but they have continued to provide information in modest compass at a reasonable price by the standards of modern academic publications.

There is no intention of departing from the principles of the first decade. Each book aims to survey findings and discussion in an important field of economic or social history that has been the subject of recent lively debate. It is meant as an introduction for readers who are not themselves professional researchers but who want to know what the discussion is all about — students, teachers and others generally interested in the subject. The authors, rather than either taking a strongly partisan line or suppressing their own critical faculties, set out the arguments and the problems as fairly as they can, and attempt a critical summary and explanation of them from their own judgement. The discipline now embraces so wide a field in the study of the human past that it would be inappropriate for each book to follow an identical plan, but all volumes will normally contain an extensive descriptive bibliography.

The series is not meant to provide all the answers but to help readers to see the problems clearly enough to form their own conclusions. We shall never agree in history, but the discipline will be well served if we know what we are disagreeing about, and why.

T. C. SMOUT
Editor

University of Edinburgh

1 Introduction

THE years between 1780 and 1850 saw fundamental changes in
social relationships in Britain which were associated with that
acceleration in economic and technological change which historians since Toynbee have called the industrial revolution. The
impact of these changes was great enough to create a new
vocabulary. 'Industry', 'factory', 'strikes', 'statistics', 'scientist' and
'railway' all came into common use or developed new meanings
during that period [R. Williams, 1958: 13; Hobsbawm, 1962: 17].
The most important of these innovations was the language of class
[Briggs, 1960]. The language of 'ranks' and 'orders' which
belonged to the writing of Gregory King, Daniel Defoe, Archdeacon Paley and Edmund Burke recognised social inequality and
graded men into a hierarchy which was linked by 'chains' and
'bonds'. The use of this language implied an acceptance of
inequality. Paley accepted the existence of these ranks as the will of
God. Each rank and station had its own duties and rights. The rich
had the right to power and property and the obligation to care for
the poor. 'To abolish riches', he wrote, 'would not be to abolish
poverty; but on the contrary, to leave it without protection or
resource.' After 1780 this language was slowly replaced by the
language of class, which first appeared among the philosophers
Millar and Gisbourne. By the 1830s and 1840s, in the writings and
speeches of Henry Hetherington, Feargus O'Connor, Richard
Cobden and John Bright, 'working classes', 'middle classes' and
'aristocracy' had become part of a language which recognised
social conflict centred on the clash of interests which arose from the
distribution of wealth, income and power. This addition to the
language does not imply that social conflict was a new feature of
British society. It does suggest that the nature and intensity of
conflict was changing, and that the manner in which men thought
about that conflict also changed.

In 1832 Dr James Kay, physician to the Ardwick and Ancoats
Dispensary, an Edinburgh-trained doctor who had learned his
political economy and evangelical religion at the feet of the
Scottish divine Thomas Chalmers, looked across a Manchester in

which 874 people out of a population of 142,000 had just died of cholera, and the Reform Bill agitation had aroused hostile middle- and working-class organisations. He wrote:

> Between the manufacturers of the country, staggering under the burdens of an enormous taxation and a restricted commerce; between them and the labouring classes subjects of controversy have arisen, and consequent animosity too generally exists. The burdens of trade diminish the profits of capital, and the wages of labour: but bitter debate arises between the manufacturers and those in their employ, concerning the proper division of that fund, from which these are derived. The bargain for the wages of labour develops organized associations of the working classes, for the purpose of carrying on the contest with the capitalist. . . . a gloomy spirit of discontent is engendered, and the public are not unfrequently alarmed, by the wild outbreak of popular violence . . . [Kay, 1832:9].

The radical journalists, like Henry Hetherington, who sought to lead working-class opinion had a very different perspective, but his social landscape was much the same: inequality, especially between labour and capitalists, conflict between them, especially over wages, and a lack of control over the extent of that conflict. It was a long way from the calm certainties of Archdeacon Paley.

What was the nature of the change which Kay perceived? If Marx was right and 'the history of all hitherto existing society is the history of class struggles', then a full account would involve a comprehensive social history of the industrial revolution, perhaps even of western capitalism. Instead we shall select *some* of the major themes in the literature to show ways in which historians have written about class, the evidence they selected, and the concepts and questions they used to interpret that evidence. The aim is not to produce an account of what happened, or even a survey of the literature parcelling it up into schools of thought, lined up in historical debates, but to create an awareness of the choices of evidence, of concepts, of questions, and of values and ideological approaches, which must be made in writing the history of class.

Marx still dominates. Even historians who reject the Marxist answers, like Perkin and Musson, are still attracted by the questions set by Marx, on the importance of social conflict, its relationship to economic change, and to the change in workplace relationships and living-standards. Hence we begin with a detailed examination of an anti-Marxist (Perkin) and the historical ideas of Marx himself before giving an account of the different models of class structure, and the different focus historians have given to events, institutions and class consciousness. All these are still areas of debate between right- and left-wing historians, as is the relationship of class development with economic change. This discussion, like the literature from which it was derived, continually returns to the themes raised by Marx. The last part of the present book suggests two alternatives for those who wish to escape from the conceptual grip of Marx, neo-Marx and anti-Marx: first the radical development of Marx's ideas in the twentieth century by the Italian Communist Gramsci, and secondly the sociological concepts inspired by Weber, both of which can help our understanding of class in the industrial revolution.

2   The 'Birth of Class'?

THE *Origins of Modern English Society* [Perkin, 1969] has been attacked for its loose formulation of the concept of class, and its claim that class society was created in a short and reasonably well defined period of time in the five years after 1815. (See *Times Literary Supplement*, 17.4.69 and the reply 1.5.69.) Perkin's book is still an excellent starting-point for thinking about the way historians use the concept of class, for that concept was the central organising principle of the book, and was carefully defined at several points in the book, as were the conclusions about social relationships which were derived from its use.

British society before the industrial revolution was according to Perkin 'a classless hierarchy', 'an open aristocracy based on property and patronage' [Perkin, 1969: 17]. There were huge inequalities, a large number of finely graded status rankings, and stable relationships between the ranks. Inequality was accepted because the higher ranks took paternalistic responsibility for the welfare of the poor. Perkin offered two ways of accommodating within the 'classless society' those conflicts which did occur in the eighteenth century over the distribution of wealth and power. 'Class', he said, 'was indeed latent in the 18th century' and was 'ruthlessly suppressed' (pp. 26, 176). He drew a clear contrast: 'Nor was it [eighteenth-century society] like the Victorian, a class society, divided by mutually hostile layers each united by a common source of income . . .' (p. 26); 'A class society is characterized by class feeling, that is by the existence of vertical antagonism between a small number of horizontally integrated groups.' Most eighteenth-century conflicts were 'horizontal antagonism between vertical interest pyramids, each embracing practically the whole range of status levels from top to bottom of society' (p. 176). The mutually hostile layers he defined by their common source of income, namely rent, profit or wages, after the manner of Adam Smith and Ricardo. Perkin then related these sources of income to particular social groups which were then further defined by an 'ideal'. This 'ideal' created within a class, a consciousness of itself, its interests, its conflicts with others, and the needs, possibilities and aims of organisation. At this point in the book (p. 219), he changed the whole focus of his concept of class from the struggle over the distribution of income to the 'struggle between ideals'. The four ideals were: (i) the aristocratic or paternalistic; (ii) the entrepreneurial middle-class belief in free competition and the virtues of the self-made man against the corruption of aristocratic government; (iii) a weakly formulated working-class ideal based on co-operation and the labour theory of value; and (iv) the professional ideal. Perkin claimed that since the professional men's middle-class incomes were independent of market forces, they were able to develop their own ideal of efficiency and service to the rest of the community. Perkin followed the struggle of ideals, not through the battle for economic power, but through the battle for the control of the state, through parliamentary and administrative reform, the new poor law, education, public health, army and civil service. The end of this was the domination of the entrepreneurial ideal temper-ed a little by the professional, as the basis of a viable class society.

There are a number of difficulties with this account. The first is the term 'latent'. If it means that class feeling occasionally emerged in the 'form of industrial and political insubordination' and was suppressed, then such 'feeling' could only have arisen from the experience, at some level, of class conflict, and the suppression must have involved one class (a ruling class) acting against another. 'Latent' was essential for the idea of the 'birth of class' for it accommodated eighteenth-century conflicts whilst reserving the concept of class for a specific series of events which then became the 'birth of class'.

By dividing English society into wage, profit and rent takers, Perkin equated a model devised by Adam Smith and Ricardo to explain the distribution of returns to factors of production in an economic system with a model of socio-economic groups to explain the distribution of wealth and power within the social system. Status divisions within classes were recognised by Perkin, but he ignored groups which derived income from a variety of factors of production, such as the land-owning industrialist, the self-employed craftsman, and the profit-seeking cottage-owning shopkeeper common in many towns. The switch of focus from source of income to 'ideal' implied that each ideal could be identified with its equivalent source of income. If individuals or minority groups deviated from this equivalence, it would not affect claims about the major direction of British society. The assumption cannot be accepted when the bulk of the eighteenth-century aristocracy were profit-seeking, custom-ignoring entrepreneurs, developing and enclosing their agricultural estates, and when a major part of the nineteenth-century middle class sought a paternalistic relationship with the lower classes, not just in the exceptional situation of the factory village, but also through countless charitable organisations.

The switch of focus concentrated attention on the 'struggle of ideals' which resolved into the 'viable class society' of the 1850s. This focus ignored changes in economic and power relationships between social classes through the development of trades-union conflict with employers, the changing use of police and army, the implications of religious and educational activity, and the creation of the banking system of 1844 and the stock exchange for the concentration of finance capital. The importance attributed to increasing scale in human organisation drew attention to the increase in population, the increased size of towns and of workplaces, but drew attention away from changes in the *relationships* of production, the changing market position of labour, and the development of new methods of work discipline. More seriously, this method failed to examine the relationship between the creation of the 'ideals' and the changing social relationships of the industrial revolution.

We must now examine, in the light of evidence of eighteenth-century conflict, the notion of 'the birth of class', with its attendant ideas of 'latent class', 'one-class society' and 'classlessness'.

The power structure of eighteenth-century Britain was dominated by a ruling class of great landowners, a 'federation of country houses', which controlled national government through a subtle mixture of patronage, deference and economic power. The Lowthers in Cumberland and the Lambtons in Durham gained the votes of tradesmen and tenants not so much from the fear of eviction and exclusive dealing but from a natural deference which identified the interests of their landlord with the prosperity and stability of the locality. The whole structure was bound together at national level by a system of bribery, jobs and contracts perfected by the Duke of Newcastle at mid-century. At local level the main institution of their power was the magistrate's bench. Here they supervised the Poor Law, regulated the militia, licensed alehouses, as well as passed judgement on theft, disorder and damage to property.

An open land market meant that new wealth did not challenge old, but simply bought a landed estate. Thus at the end of the seventeenth century, when the debt-burdened estates of the Duke of Buckingham were sold, the Yorkshire portion was bought by the banking family of Duncombe, and the Burley estate was purchased by Daniel Finch with the fortune which legal and political success had brought his father in Stuart London.[1] Defoe recognised the pattern: 'trade and learning have been the two chief steps by which our gentlemen have raised their relations and built fortunes' (*The Complete English Tradesman*, 1726). At the same time the younger sons of landowners were joining the sons of urban tradesmen and master manufacturers among the merchants and professional men, thus strengthening the social bonds between landed and other forms of economic and social power.

The strength and dominance of this aristocracy, and its ability to maintain its power as well as an open relationship with other ranks in terms of recruitment and patronage, have always impressed historians. Augustan calm has been compared with the 'progress', 'struggle' and 'conflict' of the nineteenth century. Looking forward from the seventeenth century Peter Laslett suggested that England was a 'one-class society', by which he meant that only one class, the aristocracy, was capable of 'concerted action over the whole area of society'. He defined a class as a number of people banded together to exercise collective power, political and economic, and warned that it had been the confusion of status groups (the ranks and orders of King, Paley and the rest) with social class (as he had defined it) which had obscured the one-class nature of society. His use of class was tempting. The aristocracy was the only group provided with an ideology (a mixture of Locke and the settlement of 1688), and its institutions – parliament, the church and the magistrate's bench – were an integrated whole which maintained and justified aristocratic power over the whole of England and Wales and most of Scotland and Ireland. No other group could compete with the extent and effectiveness of this ideological and institutional organisation [Laslett, 1971: *23–54*].

The concept of the 'one-class society' does have serious problems. If class was a relationship of inequality and exploitation then a 'one-class society' was a contradiction in terms, for at least two classes were required for such a relationship to exist. The contrast between a 'class for itself' and a 'class in itself' (for which see below, p. 24) is more relevant here than the contrast of class and status. Another problem arose from the qualification, 'the whole area of society'. What area did class ideology and organisation have to encompass before class formation could be acknowledged? Could class formation take place in one region? Could class attitudes and loyalties influence a limited range of relationships? If such partial influences are dismissed as not being really a 'class' society, then such a society can hardly be said to exist before the end of the nineteenth century.

How useful is the idea that eighteenth-century society was 'classless', even with Perkin's qualification that class was 'latent'? This recognition of the potential for class development in the inequality and exploitation of the eighteenth-century economy implied that little consciousness of the opposition of interests existed, in contrast to the nineteenth century with its trades unions, Chartism and Anti-Corn Law League. Although the 'classless' eighteenth century is a familiar starting-point for social histories of the industrial revolution, its existence must be questioned first by evidence of several forms of organised opposition to legitimate authority based upon social and economic interest, and designed to promote those interests in accordance with a shared system of values which were the prototype of ideology, and second, by an examination of the language of social conflict in the eighteenth century.

Organised opposition to authority took several forms. The grain riots were the best documented. In times of high prices following poor harvest, the 'law-giving mob' attacked markets, grain carts and flour mills to enforce a popular notion of 'fair prices' which they inherited from the dying paternalistic legislation of the Assize of Bread. Riots against the cider tax and militia levies opposed other forms of ruling-class action. In London, where the crowd had the chance of directly intimidating parliament, they supported Wilkes and the apprenticeship laws of the Spitalfields weavers. Their violence was disciplined and limited to specific targets. It carried the resentment and suspicion of the poor against the rich but never acted to overturn existing social arrangements, only to adjust them in favour of the poor [E. P. Thompson, 1971; Rudé, 1964].

Another potential form of opposition came from the merchant communities of the growing towns. The petitions in support of

Wilkes in the 1760s came from Bristol and Liverpool as well as from the lesser merchants and traders of London. Like the smaller freeholders of the counties who resented the growing power monopoly of the great magnates, these groups recognised their common interest in Wilkes's campaign to reduce the authority of the ruling class in government. It was rare that the opportunities of politics and resentment against tax changes, war policies or falling rents brought merchants, tradesmen and freeholders together. Usually their behaviour did fit the vertical relationship of interest groups. Bristol sugar, Liverpool slaves, the East India and City interests petitioned parliament as need arose, or worked through the great landlords, as the Leeds woollen merchants did through Fitzwilliam and Lascelles[2] [Briggs, 1959(a): 116—17].

Widespread organisation and extensive strike action in many parts of the eighteenth-century labour force in which labour and the ownership of capital were distinct were a direct challenge to the Laslett—Briggs—Perkin account of eighteenth-century society. In 1767, the Spitalfields weavers fought the breakdown of their 'Book of Prices' with a bitter and violent strike and parliament responded with an Act (1774) which empowered magistrates to fix minimum wages [S. and B. Webb, 1919: *34—41*]. Eighteenth-century class-based organisation probably went further in the north-east of England than in any other part of the country. The keelmen who loaded the colliers bound for London took effective strike action in several 'mutinies'. At the start of the century they formed their own charity, the keelmen's hospital, to take care of their aged and infirm and hotly disputed control with the Hostmen's Company, the employers' organisation. Colliers and coal owners were in continuous conflict. Both were capable of taking concerted action to limit the power of the other. In the most important strike, that of 1765, the miners defeated an attempt by the owners to replace the annual bond with a perpetual contract which would have reduced the miners to the serf status of the Scottish miners. The strike issue involved attempted changes in the legitimate power relationship of the two sides and was not just a matter of wage bargaining. In 1740 colliers and keelmen merged in the food riots which engulfed Newcastle. The 'mob' was first promised reduced prices and then fired on by troops. They finished by ransacking Newcastle Guildhall [Rudé, 1964]. The north-east even produced the beginnings of an ideological challenge to the existing distribution of power in the writing of Thomas Spence. If class society began in England, it began in the keels and mines of the Tyne and not in the cotton mills of Lancashire.

The weavers, miners and keelmen had none of the permanent bureaucratic institutions characteristic of modern labour organisation. The basic unit of organisation was the sick or burial club. These often drew members from one occupation or workplace and were loosely linked by the practice of tramping. Members of one club supported those from another one of the same occupation whilst they travelled the country looking for work. Indeed markets, hiring fairs, travelling tinkers as well as tramping must have substantially reduced the isolation which is sometimes attributed to members of the eighteenth-century labour force. These links were slender compared to the steam-press newspaper, the railway and the electric telegraph which aided the cohesion of nineteenth-century social classes. Evidence of the behaviour and consciousness of the eighteenth-century labour force is fragmentary, but it is enough to leave a question-mark against the 'classlessness' of the eighteenth century.

The language of class, the change from ranks to 'classes' (plural) raised another set of problems for 'classlessness'. Behavioural evidence suggested that semantic change was associated with social change. The evidence presented by Briggs [1960] demonstrated a change from classlessness to class, from consensus to conflict. The behaviour of the grain mobs, trades unions and merchants suggested that the change may have been from one sort of conflict to another. Comparing the language of ranks and orders with the language of class as used by Carlyle, Cobden, Hetherington and the Political Unions and Chartists is not to compare like with like. It is a comparison of the eighteenth-century discussion of status groups with the nineteenth-century discussion of conflict groups or classes. The real comparison must be with the language of 'gentlemen', 'the people' and 'the mob' for this was the eighteenth-century language of social conflict.

During the sixteenth and seventeenth centuries these words emerged with new meanings. A 'gentleman' came from the higher ranks of society, or at least had the habits of life of such a station. He could 'live idly and without manual labour' for his independence was secured by a substantial rent roll, or by professional fees and stipends. He might display his courage in field sports, or his generosity through charities, and his discrimination in architecture and painting. His position was a mixture of wealth and breeding.

18

The division between gentlemen and others was the division between those who had a share of legitimate power and those who did not. That share might be the ownership of a parliamentary borough, a justice's commission or the benefits of a tenuous family link [Perkin, 1969: 55–6; Laslett, 1971: 27]. The 'people' were those outside that power structure, but who had a claim to take a responsible part in the political process. That claim varied from the right to have their interests considered to the demand for a vote. The 'people' excluded the 'mob' and the nobility, but the exact membership of this prototype class was a matter of political debate. For Harrington writing in 1656, Defoe in 1702 and Alderman Beckford in 1761 the 'people' included yeomen, manufacturers, merchants and freeholders, men whose property gave them an interest in good government. Wilkes in his more rhetorical moments included the day labourer whose interest in the community was based upon 'the very price and value of every day's hard labour'. Paine and his followers went further and claimed an orderly constitutional share in government for all adult males.[3] The 'people' were probably equivalent to the wide and finely graded status ranges of the middle ranks which Perkin showed were over fifty per cent of the eighteenth-century population.

The 'mob' grew from the 'rabble' and should never be dismissed as the disorderly part of the population led by the idle and criminal. The mob acted with violence but rarely without some purpose determined by their own code of values (see above, p. 16). The ruling class responded with a mixture of fear and respect, concession and repression which earned the 'mob' the grudging title of the 'fourth estate' in mid-century [Rudé, 1964].

We now associate class with a tripartite image of society and certain features of industrial capitalism, factories, large-scale finance and large units of production, with trades unions and capitalists, and with socialism and laissez-faire. The balance between wages and profits is the basis of exploitation. It was clear from the writing of Spence and Paine that they regarded rent and taxation as the major means by which wealth was concentrated in the hands of the upper and middle ranks of society. Many conflicts reflect this. The price of grain contained a rent element as well as the merchant's profit. The merchant's opposition to government was usually organised over taxation. In many cases the labour–capital relationship included a rent element, as with the framework knitters who lost their independence, not to a wages bargain, but to the putter-out who collected the frame rent.

There is a tendency in the literature to look for the birth of class as a sharp change. Increasing knowledge of the eighteenth century is likely to emphasise that class formation was a slow process, originating with the emergence of the gentleman in the sixteenth century, the passing of the Statute of Artificers and the development of the Poor Law. Each crisis – Wilkes, Paine, Luddism, Parliamentary Reform and Chartism – highlighted underlying changes in economic and social organisation, in consciousness and in the ability of regions and interests to co-operate with each other, but like the booms and slumps of industrial growth none of them marked a major discontinuity in social behaviour.

3 Marx

W E are left through the writing of men like Kay, Hetherington and Carlyle with a sense of great and disruptive change taking place, which cannot be eliminated merely by showing the inadequacies of the three class, neo-Ricardian model, and of the notion of 'the birth of class'. How else can these changes be described and analysed? Karl Marx is a major social historian in his own right, and it is reasonable to expect considerable assistance from ideas developed as a result of close study of the industrial revolution. For the social historian, the writings of Marx should be approached as a massive workbench for social history rather than as a contentious document of political philosophy.

Marx offered a direct and all-embracing scheme for the study of society:

> In the social production which men carry on they enter into definite relations that are indispensable and independent of their will; these relations of production correspond to a definite state in the development of their material powers of production. The sum total of these relations of production constitutes the economic structure of society – the real foundation on which rise legal and political superstructures and to which correspond definite forms of social consciousness. (Preface to *Critique of Political Economy*)

Marx invited an examination of the relationships between (i) the development of technology: textile machinery, the growing efficiency of the steam engine, the improving quality of metals, (ii) relationships of production: the size of the labour force in any given unit of production, the degree of contact with the owners, the size and organisation of markets for capital, for commodities and for labour, (iii) the legal and political superstructures: parliament, political parties and pressure groups, trades unions, the police, army and institutions of religion and education, and (iv) 'social consciousness'.

Marx makes clear that he considers (iii) and (iv) the dependent variables. Labour — the creative interaction of man and nature — is the basis of society. The nature of political conflict and action depends upon economic conflict and structure. Social consciousness, which in its highly developed form becomes ideology, was created by social groups in the course of their experience of economic relationships, and may well be used through political, legal and cultural organisation to influence future changes in the relationships of production. Thus the ideas of the political economists influenced middle- and ruling-class attitudes to trades unions, Corn Laws and the legal control of prices and wages. In recent years Marxist writers have paid much more attention to the influence of the feedback of ideas and ideology upon economic relationships.

Marx considered that the class structure of Britain was a result of the economic relationships of the capitalist mode of production. This originated in the sixteenth century and came to dominate the economy over the succeeding two centuries. Its distinctive features were the private ownership of the means of production, the use of this for profit seeking, and a money exchange economy. Relationships depended, in Carlyle's phrase, upon the 'cash nexus'. Social relationships became market relationships without the mutual if unequal obligations of feudalism. The spread of capitalism through the expropriation of peasant rights in the land (which created an urban labour force); the creation of a cash market for food in the towns and the expansion of manufactures through foreign trade was a slow process. This was accelerated at the end of the eighteenth century by the increasing freedom of market relationships from legal control, by the increasing pace of technological change, and most important of all, by the growth of large-scale industry. 'The history of the English working classes', wrote Engels in 1844, 'begins in the last half of the eighteenth century, with the invention of the steam engine and the machines for manufacturing cotton' [Engels, 1845: 9].

The class structure created by these economic relationships was dominated by the bourgeoisie (the owners and controllers of capital) and by the proletariat (those who had no property in the means of production and who lived by selling their labour in a free market). The relationship between these two classes was one of conflict and dependence. Their identity, like the identity of other classes, did not depend solely on their source of income. Ricardo's division of society into the takers of rent, profits or wages was too simple. The economic relationships of class were linked to political domination. The dominant class exploited the subordinate class through the expropriation of the surplus product of their labour, leaving just enough, allowing for temporary deviations caused by market conditions, for labour to feed and reproduce itself. This domination was achieved under a system of laws created by the state, and maintained by main force and ideological influence. In this context Perkin's problem with the professions may be resolved. The bulk of the professions were a specialised sector of the ruling class which dealt with key aspects of economic and political domination: the lawyers with property, the church with ideology, the military officers with main force, and the medical men with the health of the producers of wealth as well as the health of the dominant class.

Although Marx based his analysis of society upon the relationship between the two great classes of exploiters and exploited, capital and labour, rulers and ruled, he recognised that at any given moment in history there existed several intermediate classes. They existed for several reasons. Some survived from previous modes of production, like the master craftsman who provided both capital and labour for the small unit of production which he controlled. Other classes, like the crofter of Highland Scotland, or the vast numbers of casual labourers, paupers, beggars and criminals (the *lumpenproletariat*), were part of the dynamic of capitalism and shared common economic interests, but for a variety of reasons took only an indirect part in the major class conflict between capital and labour. Conflict based on common economic interest took place within the major social classes, which were by no means homogeneous. The struggles of landed and industrial capital split the bourgeoisie, and the clashes between skilled craftsmen and casual labour divided the proletariat. Marx did not claim that Britain was a two-class society. What he did claim was that the conflict between labour and capital was the most important of all the conflicts within society (including non-economic ones) and that this conflict was the dominant influence in the distribution of wealth and power. The Irish and Scottish labourers might fight on the railway contracts over Shap Fell but they both joined the same strikes and both bargained for wages on the same side of the labour market. Landowners and industrialists might clash over the Corn Laws, but they all cooperated to exclude the labouring classes from political and industrial power.

Marx believed that several trends in nineteenth-century British society were characteristic of capitalist society in general. He believed that these trends were dependent on the relationship between labour and capital and would end with the fundamental revolutionary change of capitalist society. He saw an increase in the concentration of industrial capital, in the speed of technological change and in the intensity of competition. This would force the intermediate classes, the master craftsmen, the shopkeepers and the lesser professional men to sink into the proletariat and would progressively eliminate differences of skill and prestige within the working class itself. At the same time aristocratic power would be eliminated in conflict with the bourgeoisie. Thus society was polarised into two classes.

Political and economic domination would increase the gap between the two classes, and competition would force down the relative standard of living of the working classes (the 'immiseration of the proletariat'). This view is sharply outlined in the *Communist Manifesto*, but in the more detailed account in *Capital* the process of immiseration is mitigated by the enlightened self-interest of the bourgeois factory acts. At the same time the accumulation of capital and the divorce of production from consumption would cause declining profits and increasingly severe crises of trade. These two factors would lead to a final crisis in which the proletariat, driven by increased suffering, joined by elements of a disorganised bourgeoisie, would radically transform the nature of society. At this point social history ends and politics begins.

Marx's account of the development of industrial society contained two distinct uses of the term 'class'. One referred to the major classes of industrial society and the other to the intermediate classes of industrial society which existed in any given historical situation.

He made another important distinction between 'class in itself' and 'class for itself'. Of the first he wrote: 'In so far as millions of families live under economic conditions which separate their way of life, their interests and their education from those of other classes and oppose them to these, they constitute a class.' (*The Eighteenth Brumaire of Louis Bonaparte*) All class situations produced inequalities in the life chances of different social groups. Historians reflect this in their studies of death rates, housing conditions, education and religious behaviour. But those involved, especially the subordinate groups, often had little awareness of what was happening, and still less of the organisation and ideology needed to oppose those who profited from their disadvantage. Such class relationships were passive. The Highlander might resist the clearances, and the urban poor be driven to theft by their hunger, but such actions lacked direction and any awareness of the economic and social causes of distress. Indeed many may consider that the conflicts of the eighteenth century took this form. The concept of 'class in itself' has much in common with Perkin's 'latent' class conflict. Class formation needed to go further than this before it had the important social results Marx expected: 'In so far as the identity of their interests does not produce a community, national associations and political organization – they do not constitute a class.' (*Eighteenth Brumaire*)

The largest section of the literature of class in the industrial revolution examines the growth of awareness by the middle and working classes through trades unions, political parties, voluntary organisations and pressure groups. It was the accelerating pace of class formation, class action and class relationships at this level which produced that sense of disruptive social change which pervaded the period. These organisations and the clashes they produced in turn moulded social consciousness into a class ideology, a system of thought which interpreted the industrial world in a way which informed each class of its own true interests, and guided them to actions and organisation designed to change relationships of production in a manner which benefited the class concerned.

But in the course of the nineteenth century the class structure and conflict in Britain tended to become more complex rather than to simplify in the manner Marx suggested. A new labour aristocracy replaced the old artisan craft élite. Marginal groups like shopkeepers and schoolteachers grew in numbers without being assimilated in one of the major social classes. Joint stock companies and large growing government agencies increased the size of the managerial and administrative class, men of power who did not own capital. The sophistication of science increased the size of professional groups like doctors and engineers, and the aristocracy survived to provide leadership in domestic, foreign and eventually imperial policy.

Reading Marx leaves us with a more complex and flexible notion of class and better able to return to the historical literature to examine the manner in which the basic changes in social relationships during the industrial revolution have been discussed.

4 Institutions and Events

NOW, class appears in the history books as (i) groups of people, (ii) institutions, (iii) a set of events, (iv) a form of consciousness, and as (v) an account of changing relationships between groups of people.

The terminology of class is used by many historians in a descriptive sense. It is used as a classification system to show the distribution of social fortune and behaviour patterns among different groups in the community. Death rates, morbidity, age of marriage, housing types, education, religious behaviour, drinking habits, leisure and dress have all been shown to differ between social groups which historians have labelled classes. Such labels have enormous descriptive value but little theoretical or dynamic content. The groups they describe have more in common with status groups than with the central problems of the conflict over the distribution of wealth and power, of class consciousness and of ideology.

It is unfair to dismiss this use of class as descriptive. The terminology of class is chosen for this task because it refers to the systems which distribute rewards in society, wealth, income, education, health and so on. The inequalities of class produce differences in rewards which are often interrelated (housing, income and health for example) and which produce differential social and cultural behaviour in matters as varied as sex and church-going [Smout, in MacLaren, 1976; Wickham, 1957]. These differences in turn often serve to perpetuate the inequalities. With the exception of the literature on nineteenth-century education, historians rarely developed the argument to this point. The student must accept the descriptive information as valuable raw material, and seek for himself the systems of distribution, the causes of differentiation within the class system, and the manner (if any) in which these differences perpetuate inequality. (See Stedman Jones [1971] for an example of descriptive information used in theoretical and dynamic argument.)

Another major part of the literature of class is concerned with institutions. Institutions have played a crucial role in class history, but their dominance has tended until recently to distort that history. Because such literature tends to be written about surviving institutions, especially trades unions, it creates a whiggish impression of class history, small beginnings and struggles followed by slow development leaving behind primitive violence and millennial dreams (like those of the GNCTU in 1834 seeking to transform society through a general strike). The process ended with legal recognition, tolerance from employers, wider membership and a recognised constitutional place in society [Pelling, 1963]. In a recent survey of the massive literature on trades unions Musson asserts that 'humdrum matters, relating to wages, hours, apprenticeships etc.' were of more fundamental importance than revolutionary movements. As he admits later, the study of union records tends to emphasise sectional concerns and not class aspirations [Musson, 1972: *11*, *64*]. For Cole and Postgate [1938] trades unions were 'natural instruments of conflict'. So they were, but their study should not divert attention from other means by which occupational groups defended their rights against employers. There were traditional even semi-magical means, like the Society of the Horseman's Word in north-east Scotland whose members like horsemen in other grain-growing areas could control their horses by drawing and jading oils known only to themselves. If they wished they could make the horses impossible to control when an awkward master gave unreasonable orders [Carter, in MacLaren, 1976]. There were less formally organised structures like the respectable behaviour patterns of many artisans. Through the habits of saving, sobriety and self-control which this behaviour gave them, and through the prestige they gained in the eyes of certain sections of the ruling class, the artisans were better able to defend their economic position against their employers [Gray, 1976].

Organisations which represent the pre-history of our own political culture, like the Owenite socialists and the co-operative movement, have received considerable attention, but other means of class organisation, like the Friendly Societies, have had less. Friendly Societies had a far wider nineteenth-century membership than any other organisational form including the trades unions yet no attempt has been made to distil the aspirations of the members from the countless rule books which survive in local collections.[4] There is a general neglect of employers and middle-class organisations with the exception of the Anti-Corn Law League

[McCord, 1958]. There are histories of Chambers of Commerce and Literary and Philosophical Societies, but most such histories ignore the place these organisations had in class history. The employers and middle-class sponsors for whom most of these histories were written like to believe that class conflict had a minor place in British history, and such organisations were less prepared to identify themselves as class organisations than were the trades unions. Hence the danger that in a general survey (such as this) the impression will be given that class formation and class consciousness were matters for the working classes only. Both middle and ruling class (defined here as that which controlled the means of government and the means of production) had complex and influential class institutions and ideologies.

Class is no more a series of events than it is a social structure or a social institution; nevertheless the bulk of the literature on class examines a key series of events.

The individual awareness of class and of class relationships was and is created through a host of incidents in schools, home, work, shops or in the observation of habits of speech, dress and manners. Any expression of class feeling is a summary of countless, often ordinary experiences. Arthur Munby, minor poet, civil servant, and son of a Yorkshire landed family, was acutely aware of the details of class distinction for he courted and married a servant girl, a maid of all work. Courtship was not easy: 'She would not take my arm – for it was still daylight and many people were about – . . . she hung back and whispered, "You know I have no gloves".' Visual signals like this continually divided classes. A woman without gloves was no lady, especially if she was seen walking arm-in-arm down the street with a gentleman.[5] In 1851, the *Christian Socialist* printed an anonymous account of 'How I became a Chartist rebel'. The writer, a respectable but unemployed working man, visited the local Mendicity Society, was insulted by the board of gentlemen, and found that the 'rules' forbad him to take his bread and cheese home to share with his family. That evening he became a Chartist [D. Thompson, 1971: *82–6*].

Although most class experience consisted of such incidents of humiliation and superiority which confirmed each individual's sense of his own class, historians, like those who wish to organise and lead class-based groups, need more than this to assert class identity. They tend to choose experiences in common, key symbolic events and ideological concepts.

Historians, by the nature of their trade, tend to recount class as a series of key events. Class in the industrial revolution is seen as beginning with the publication of Paine's *The Rights of Man* and the political activity and repression which followed. The Nore mutiny, the Luddites and protests against the Orders in Council, the Blanketeers, Peterloo, the Queen Caroline affair and the repeal of the Combination Acts take the story into the mid 1820s. The 1830s open with the Swing riots, the 1832 Reform Act, the passing of the New Poor Law and the campaign of the unstamped press. Chartism and the Anti-Corn Law League dominate the 1840s, and the rise of the new model unions the following decade.

On individual events historians disagree. On 16 August 1819 the Manchester Yeomanry rode into a massive crowd attending a radical meeting in St Peter's Fields, Manchester. Their aim was to arrest Henry Hunt and other radical leaders addressing the meeting. To do this they dispersed the crowd with sabres drawn, killing eleven and injuring some 500 more. For E. P. Thompson [1963] this was an act of open class aggression; for Donald Read [1958] the tragic result of the gap and lack of understanding between social classes in Manchester; and for Robert Walmsley, who has set the event in local context, it was the understandable response by the authorities to very real fears of revolution. [6] Whatever the correct verdict, none of the three disputed the importance of the event, and nothing can alter the fact that Peterloo became a potent symbol of the repression of the 'people'. It was condemned at mass meetings in most major cities, thus heightening the awareness of this social division in a way that personal experience could never do. The 'butchers' of Manchester appeared in radical literature and on reform banners for several decades after 1819.

In many histories of class the events listed here appear like the battle honours of the working-class movement: most class histories are written as histories of the working class [e.g. Cole and Postgate, 1938; S. and B. Webb, 1919]. The whiggish dimension was clear in these Fabian histories. Each event raised the level of working-class consciousness, driving the working class towards an institutionalised, constitutionalised and powerful place in British society. Indeed some historians and at least one sociologist see the progress of the nineteenth century not as an institutionalisation of class conflict, but as a continuous process of claims for civil rights which were progressively granted [Marshall, 1950].

Much of the literature of class contains detailed discussion of one or more of these organisations or events. Most of the events were conflict situations. Most of the organisations and movements were involved in conflict situations. Certain questions tend to recur. What social groupings were represented in these conflicts? With which groups did men of various social and economic backgrounds identify themselves? What sort of social relationships existed between such groups? We have already begged the question by assuming conflict of some nature. There are three realistic alternative forms of relationship: first deference, the acceptance of subordination as legitimate, as in the eighteenth-century landlord-tenant relationship; second co-operation in which values and aims were shared by socio-economic groups, but where, despite inequality, the subordinate group retained considerable independence, as did the members of the new model unions of the 1850s; finally apathy, the last defence of those with no power cynically to ignore the efforts of their superiors to get them to participate in social relationships.[7] The widespread refusal of wage earners to attend church was one symptom of this [Wickham, 1957].

5 Which Social Groups Were Represented in Class Conflict?

THERE are two ways in which most people, historians included, talk about the major socio-economic divisions in society.

The most common way, the three-class model, has two major drawbacks (see above, pp. 12–14): (i) there was a lack of homogeneity within each of the three classes, notably in terms of source and level of income; and (ii) there was no consistent or uniform relationship between forms of social consciousness or ideology and the three classes. The existence of deviant individuals—Perkin's 'social cranks'—is not at issue here, but when large sections of each social class deviated from the class 'ideology' this presents serious problems for a terminology which implies unity within each of the three classes, upper or aristocracy, middle and working or labouring classes. The concept of 'class in itself' and 'class for itself' provides one solution to this problem (see above, p. 24, and below, p. 34).

Yet most general discussions imply a three-class model. It is the natural way to think about class in an industrial society. Asa Briggs's wide range of writing sustained this model, because he looked for those situations to which it applied, and found an increasing number in the period after 1780, and because he never claimed universality for the model. In 1834 John Stuart Mill wrote that his fellow social commentators 'revolve in their eternal circle of landlords, capitalists and labourers, until they seem to think of the distinction of society into those three classes as if it were one of God's ordinances' (*The Monthly Repository*, 1834, quoted by Briggs [1956]). Dozens of historians have followed. Even those who wish to change the system retain the terminology of three classes, amalgamating and sub-dividing according to need.

In most European social history the peasantry played a major part. As John Saville [1969] pointed out, the English economy was one of the few which entered the industrial revolution without a substantial peasant class. The historian of Scotland must retain that category for the 'gudeman' of the lowlands, who in due course became a capitalist tenant farmer, but above all for the tenants and sub-tenants of the Highlands who were turned into crofters and emigrants by the harsh pressures of rising population and the market economy. [Smout, 1969: *302–60*; Hunter, 1976]. A similar process in Ireland provided a substantial portion of the unskilled labour force for British towns and cities.

The major alternative is the two-class model proposed by Marx. E. P. Thompson [1963] and Hobsbawm [1962] both noted the political convergence of the aristocracy and the large capitalist manufacturers in the 1790s. Aristocratic and middle-class manners and politics tended to converge increasingly throughout the period. The division of industrial and aristocratic capital was unreal. The Londonderrys and Fitzwilliams as coal owners, the Calthorpes and Ramsdens as urban developers in Birmingham and Huddersfield, and the many banking and manufacturing fortunes which inter-married with landed wealth all mingled sources of income traditionally allocated to specific classes [Spring, 1951]. Capital was capital whether it was landed, commercial or industrial.

Any use of the two-class model in specific historical situations must insist on the existence of sub-classes. John Foster [1974] in his account of Oldham identified capitalists and wage labourers as the major conflict groups. He was criticised by Musson for not giving enough attention to the 'great number of small capitalists renting floors or small portions of factories' who were observed by the *Morning Chronicle* reporter when he visited Oldham in 1849. This does not discomfort Foster. He had placed tradesmen, shopkeepers and small masters in their own sub-groups. The separate identity of each group was established by an examination of marriage patterns, property holding, and activity in church, chapel and voluntary society. Foster could be criticised for giving the tradesmen and small masters subordinate status to the other two classes, but not for ignoring them.

Recently Neale [1972] offered an alternative to these with his five-class model. The mixture of error and insight in the scheme is instructive. He divided the middle class into: (i) industrial and commercial property owners with the leading professional men who were deferential and aspiring towards the upper class; and (ii) the middling class of petty bourgeoisie and lesser professional men, non-deferential and needing a radical change in the power structure of society to gain any real share of power. The working class was divided into (i) the proletariat of the factories and domestic industry, who were collectivist and non-deferential; and (ii) the agricultural labourers, domestic servants and urban poor who were deferential and dependent. The whole system failed to distinguish class divisions from status divisions within a class which produced different reactions to the class situation. What Neale had discovered was not that society consisted of five classes but that one portion of the middle class and one portion of the working class, for different reasons, did not have a developed class organisation or class consciousness. In the case of the upper-middle classes, their access to upper-class power by way of politics, marriage and the land market made this unnecessary. In the case of the poorest section of the working class, poverty and powerlessness made full class formation impossible. The Swing riots [Hobsbawm and Rudé, 1969] and the accounts by Mayhew (1862, vol. I, pp. 20, 58) of the costermongers, claiming 'we are all Chartists now' or collecting for their fellow coster whose donkey had dropped dead, suggest consciousness and mutuality enough: all they lacked was power.

This scheme drew attention to an important social grouping in British society, but failed to examine this group in any detail. There was an alliance between artisan and skilled members of the working classes and the middling class (petty bourgeoisie in Marxist terms). Although the alliance weakened after the 1790s, it has been identified as a powerful influence in the 1830s and 1840s among the radicals of London [Rowe, 1970], Leeds [Tyrell, 1970] and north-east England [Nossiter, 1975] as well as Bath [Neale, 1972]. But was this alliance based on the sort of convergence of economic and ideological interest which is essential for class formation? The ideological base of the alliance was a claim for constitutional change, but there was little economic content except a general opposition to monopoly. We know little about the possible convergence of economic interest. There was a life-cycle of social mobility from apprentice to journeyman to small master in places like Birmingham. Cottage property was owned by the artisan as well as by the small shopkeeper. Two studies of marriage patterns showed that although the middling classes were more likely to choose marriage partners from amongst themselves than amongst the working classes or upper classes, they were more likely to marry into the families of craftsmen than the families of labourers [Foster, 1974: 267–9; Gray, 1976: 112; both refer to the later part of our period].

Even if the economic and social basis of this political alliance could be clearly demonstrated, its existence might still be dismissed as having no historical role, no importance for the long-run development of British society. The trend towards the increasing power of state, industrial corporation and trades union suggests that the Painite dream of a democracy of independent producers was indeed one of the by-ways of history, yet it was transmuted into a powerful belief in democracy as a protection against oppression. As a means of salving if not solving grievances this belief ran through Chartism and the women's suffrage movement and still plays a part in modern politics.

If this alliance is established as a coherent social and economic group it is important to note that the recent analysis of occupational titles from the British census of 1851 has shown that the bulk of the population was located (in status terms) in the middling or skilled working class. (See Table I.)

Table I

Percentage of the population in each of the Registrar-General's social classes

	I	II	III	IV	V
York 1841	7·8	20·5	46·7	13·8	11·4
York 1851	7·8	14·2	51·3	13·7	13·0
Nottingham 1851	3·4	11·6	61·9	13·8	9·5

Data Source: Alan Armstrong, *Stability and change in an English County Town* (Cambridge, 1974) and Roger Smith, 'The social structure of Nottingham and adjacent districts . . .' (University of Nottingham Ph.D. thesis, 1968).

Society, then was not a pyramid but egg-shaped. This pattern depends upon the acceptance of the classification used which was an adaptation of the Registrar-General's scheme divised between 1911 and 1951. This classification is descriptive, quite different from Neale's five classes, and is noted for producing a lumpy class three. Foster used a different and wider range of criteria which included servant-keeping and property ownership as well as occupational title. (See Table II.)

Table II
Social structure of Oldham, Northampton and South Shields, 1841–1851 (percentage of totals)

	magnate, Profes- sional, tradesman	small master, clerical, shopkeeper	craft	semi- skilled	labourer, pauper
Oldham 1841	4	16	18	55	7
Oldham 1851	3	14	19	51	13
Oldham 1861	2	15	20	44	19
Northampton 1851	5	26	11	43	14
South Shields 1851	3	18	23	40	17

Data Source: Foster [1974: 76].

Here the semi-skilled dominate, a result produced partly by the different nature of the three towns and partly by the different basis of classification.

6 *What Form Did Class Consciousness Take?*

THE existence of socio-economic groups differentiated by inequality in the distribution of wealth and power, and by actual or potential conflict over the means by which that distribution was made, was only part of class history. Such inequalities exist in all but the most primitive societies. These inequalities became more important after 1780, because the middle and labouring classes began to achieve a sense of their own identity, interests and opposition to other groups: in other words a class consciousness.

It is useful to distinguish several levels of class consciousness. First there is 'consensus', the simple awareness of differences, rights and duties (see above, pp. 9 and 14). Next there is 'labour consciousness', the awareness of conflict, and of the need to protect living-standards against exploitation, and to maintain organisation to do this. This created a sense of identity within an occupational group, and sometimes with wage earners as a whole, but aspirations were limited to improvements in wages, hours and conditions within the existing social system. The politics of interest groups – coal, woollens and corn – played the same role in middle-class history. Finally, 'revolutionary class consciousness' created a sense of identity within a whole economic class, enabling the class-conscious members of that class to envisage wholesale changes in the organisation of society which would make major gains in welfare and authority for that class; and at the extreme to abolish class differences. This has usually been discussed in terms of working-class ideologies, Painite, Owenite and socialist, but the middle-class ambitions for the full implementation of Malthusian and Ricardian economic systems were equally revolutionary; indeed their partial implementation was an aspect of the events discussed here.

E. P. Thompson's *The Making of the English Working Class* is central to the literature of class in the industrial revolution. His major assertion, that between 1780 and 1832 most English working people came to feel an identity of interest among themselves and against their employers, was sustained by the presentation of class experience as a massive learning process – the learning and achieving of class consciousness.

The working people of England began learning their own identity through the experiences of the 1790s, Paine's writing, the societies which discussed his ideas, the repression of those societies and the food shortages of 1795 and 1799–1800. In 1791, people had cheerfully supplied 'church-and-king' mobs to wreck the houses and chapels of dissenters with French revolutionary sympathies – perhaps with the prompting of beer money from the tory-Anglican magistrates. After 1795 there was a sullen silence, with strong evidence of a revolutionary tradition formed by illegal and shadowy societies like the United Englishmen. Class consciousness was part of a reaction to the increased exploitation of labour that was itself part of the logic of capitalist development (see below, pp. 48–56). Expectations of fair wages and working conditions were disappointed amongst agricultural labourers, weavers and many of the skilled tradesmen of London: real wages fell, hours increased and the apprenticeship laws collapsed. After 1815 economic slump, high food prices, intense political discussion in a network of political clubs, and the suppression of that activity by the Six Acts and by the class terrorism of Peterloo, increased and spread the sense of injustice and oppression.

Working people came to this situation with three traditions to guide their action. There was the tradition of popular action to gain fair wages and prices (see above, p. 16). Then there was that of the 'free born Englishman' derived from memories of the seventeenth-century conflicts reinforced by Wilkes and Washington and crystallised by Paine. One Sheffield Jacobin decorated his walls with aquatints of Cromwell and Washington, both men who had defeated a king. Even the aristocrat-made law of the eighteenth century held the view that all men were equally subject to the law and very occasionally hanged an aristocrat to prove it [Hay et al., 1975]. Most important was the tradition of dissenting religion, which provided a focus for social activity as well as a sense of equality before God, freedom of conscience, and the experience of political struggle, for dissenters still lost important civil rights under laws designed to favour the established church. Theological debate nurtured skills easily transposed to politics. Paine was educated by Quakers and Thomas Hardy was trained in the faction fights of the English Presbyterians.

By the 1820s William Cobbett, Richard Carlile, William Hone

and others were fashioning a full-blooded attack on all forms of aristocratic authority, religious, political and economic.

The learning process took place in two ways. First there was an increased awareness of what was happening, created by experience itself and by the network of societies which developed in such profusion after 1815, like the penny-a-month club of weavers at Barnsley in 1816, formed for the purpose of buying radical newspapers [E. P. Thompson, 1963: 717]. Second there was the long and painful process of experimentation with different forms of social and political action to counter the deprivation caused by economic and political forces. The process moved from the Methodist chapel, to riots and petitions to the Luddites hanged at York and the dead of Peterloo, and at last to the working-class people who joined trades unions and political associations in the 1830s. Although Thompson has been accused of 'thirsting for bourgeoisie blood' (Chambers, *History*, 1966), the process he described was that of a working class which had lost one legitimate and stable relationship with its employers and sought another. Even Luddite anger was in part the result of the failure of traditional constitutional appeals for legal help to protect living standards. Although the seeking was often a violent and disorganised one, the achievement contained many elements of stability.

Thompson stopped deliberately in 1830. Like Hobsbawm [1962], he identified this as the point at which the English working class was responding as a class to the changes brought about by industrial capitalism. The story may be followed further by two very different books. Patricia Hollis's collection of readings showed the learning process very clearly [Hollis, 1973]. The old analysis of Paine and Cobbett, of people-versus-aristocracy, was supplemented by the new analysis of capital-versus-labour in the writing of Hodgskin, Hetherington and Ernest Jones. The unstamped press of the 1830s was an important means of self-education for the politically conscious members of the working class. The persecution of that press further developed the sense of class opposition [Hollis, 1970]. New solutions were sought by mass trades unions, by co-operators and Owenites, by dreams of general strikes and armed political uprisings, as well as by the Chartist search for the Painite democratic solution.

In *Class Struggle and the Industrial Revolution* John Foster focused attention on the Lancashire cotton textile town of Oldham to demonstrate the existence of a revolutionary mass working-class consciousness in the 1830s and 1840s. The book raised questions about the causes of such a development, and about the sort of evidence which can justify historians who talk about revolutionary class consciousness. Foster traced the means by which class relationships developed from the stability of the eighteenth century, through labour consciousness to the attitudes of the 1830s. The concentration of capital in the early cotton factories did not create class conflict. What the spinning factory did was to upset the means by which that conflict had been stabilised for over a century. Mechanisation in spinning brought down the price of yarn, so that European producers of finished goods, using British yarn and their own cheap labour, were able to undercut British cloth prices in overseas markets. Weaving was not mechanised until the 1820s, so that from the 1790s the masters could cut costs and compete only by forcing down wages. This they could do because population increase placed labour in a poor market position. Thus the wage expectations of the weavers, legitimised by experience, could not be met. The economic conflict switched from food prices, which as JPs the ruling class could control, to wages, for which as employers they could offer no palliative. In the 1830s the employers attacked the spinners' wages in the same way, but this time because of falling profits and periodic trade slumps.

Working-class response to this situation came in two phases. First, as trades-union (or labour) consciousness which involved action to defend the living-standard and bargaining position of each trade. In Oldham the trades union and radical leaders used the popular elements of local government and threats of exclusive dealing against the enfranchised members of the petty bourgeoisie to gain control of police, vestry, Poor Law and, after 1832, parliamentary representation. Some time after 1830 working-class understanding of what was happening changed to a revolutionary class consciousness. Guided, says Foster, by the community's 'revolutionary vanguard', the working class gained a mass 'intellectual conviction' that not only must they oppose the employers in day-to-day economic struggles but that a 'total change of the social system' was the only solution to their problems [Foster, 1974: 74, 99–100]. This was more than a response to poverty. Since 1816 cotton operatives had looked to legislation to limit hours and wages and thus distribute some of the benefits of machinery to labour. This early and direct involvement of politics with the labour – capital relationship made it easier for mass understanding to be led to make demands for a total change in the social system.

Comment must be made on the evidence for revolutionary class consciousness. Such evidence is difficult to come by because of its very nature. Statements by the leadership and by propagandists were there, but there were only scraps of behavioural evidence by which to judge the thoughts and ambitions of the mass of the labour force. Foster relied on the events of 1834 and 1842 for such evidence. In the early months of 1834 Oldham workers of all trades gave support to Doherty and Fielden's National Regeneration Society. In April 1834, when police raided a trades-union lodge, all the trades of Oldham came out on strike and those arrested were rescued. The strike continued for a week with support from the Manchester delegates of the Regeneration Society. The major strike aim was to enforce an eight-hour day by extra-parliamentary means. Although this was no more than an extension of demands made in 1819, the strike was seen by many of its leaders as part of a larger struggle between rich and poor, between labour and capital [Foster, 1974: *110—14*]. There was little evidence of any political planning behind the strike. True, the strike was organised and involved large numbers, but this is not necessarily evidence for anything more than a response to the attacks made by the authorities on the trades unions. The response would be made in light of the traditions and experiences of the past thirty years. (See also Stedman Jones, *New Left Review*, 1975.) Nor did the strike have 'intellectual conviction' enough to sustain it beyond the week. The Webbs dismissed it as a 'spasm of insurrection' [S. and B. Webb, 1919: *152*]. Indeed when the strike and the National Regeneration Society had collapsed, the spinners' delegates in 1835 declared, 'we would despoil no man of his rightful property; we dream not of any absolute equality of condition . . . ' [Cole, 1953: *153*]. Still, this could be seen as a tactical withdrawal, not as a loss of faith in revolutionary change.

The strike, like the Plug Plot of 1842, was clearly more than a wages struggle [Rudé, 1964]. The Oldham working class did respond with a common sense of opposition to the authority of the state and their employers but they had neither the clarity of vision nor the strength of faith in an alternative economic order to carry them forward. The Jacobin republic of the small producer had been left behind and the socialist analysis of revolutionary aims and tactics had hardly begun. Owenite ideas, Benbow's plans for a general strike and the early analysis of the exploitation of labour by capital in the unstamped press were all available in Oldham in 1834 and 1842 but there is little evidence that any of these blueprints for a revolutionary consciousness dominated the minds of the mass of the Oldham working class in those crisis years. If behavioural evidence is taken from a wider time span, then it seems that the working classes of Oldham dominated the major political institutions of the town without any serious challenge to private property or to capitalist production in the borough. Instead, a stronger bargaining position was achieved within the capitalist system of production and distribution. They openly sought more control over their relationships with their capitalist employers and gained this in a limited manner when the Ten Hours Factory Act was passed in 1847. In the absence of some ghostly interviewing technique it is impossible adequately to test any hypothesis about the existence of mass revolutionary class consciousness and be certain about the thoughts of those who filled the streets of Oldham in the crucial weeks of 1834 and 1842.

This criticism in part concerns evidence and its interpretation, but it also depends upon two assumptions about the concepts being used. The criticism assumed that a mass revolutionary class consciousness included not only opposition to the capitalist system of production but also some positive notion of the type of society which would replace that system. It is also assumed that behavioural evidence for such consciousness must be sustained over time. If these assumptions are rejected then the criticism in part falls.

Further caution arises from the relative isolation of Foster's Oldham. It lay like some cotton-spinning Cuba in the foothills of the Pennines, plotting revolution but receiving little welcome when its delegates ventured into the wider society of Britain. The Regeneration Society men met with little enthusiasm when they visited the trades unionists of the Leeds area in the 1830s. It matters not that towns like South Shields and Northampton (which Foster used for contrast) and Neale's Bath had little interest in such plans, for their economic structure made such a development unlikely. What matters is the lack of evidence for the same sort of behaviour in other textile towns. This is a caution, not a rejection. Studies of towns like Bradford and Huddersfield may produce results more compatible with Oldham, for they were also single-industry textile towns into which the military commanders in charge of internal security in the 1830s were afraid to send their troops. The relationship of Oldham and any other towns like it to the rest of the country still needs to be worked out.

There was an important contrast in the writing of Thompson and Foster. Foster talked in terms of a revolutionary vanguard leading and developing mass consciousness. This owes much to Lenin (*What is to be Done?*, 1902), who separated economic struggle based on day-to-day conflict in the workplace from the political struggle which concerned the total overthrow of the capitalist state and society. Lenin suggested forcibly that 'class political consciousness can be brought to the workers only from without, that is only from outside of the economic struggle, outside of the sphere of relationships between workers and employers.' In Oldham the role of the 'vanguard' had to be taken by a leadership drawn from the trades unions themselves and from the Jacobin politics of the French Wars. These men developed their ideas through a generation of experience and experimentation defending wage earners' living-standards. They did not need to gain access to the working-class community because they were part of it. There seems little analytical gain and much confusion to be derived from turning an active political and trades-union leadership into a 'vanguard'. E. P. Thompson recognised leaders and intellectuals as important but made no attempt to separate them in any way from the working-class community. This community was, he asserts, 'the product . . . of conscious working-class endeavour'. Friendly societies and sick clubs demanding 'decency and regularity' from members, by their philosophical claims 'that man is formed a social being', as well as by their actions, created ideals of mutuality which were central to nineteenth-century working-class culture. The community experience of work, prices, religion and leisure created class consciousness, not the vanguard [E. P. Thompson, 1963: *418–20, 613*].

There is an important counter-literature to that represented by Thompson, Foster and Hollis. This denies the existence of any mass class consciousness of a revolutionary or even of a fundamentally conflict-orientated kind. There are three major lines of attack in this literature.

The first is best summarised in the words of a recent chairman of a Glasgow Rangers supporters club: 'It's only a small minority of troublemakers . . . '. Geoffrey Best asked of *The Making of the*

43

English Working Class, where was the flag-saluting, foreigner-hating, drunken, wife-beating working man? (*Historical Journal*, 1965). There are two Marxist answers to this: (i) in the *lumpenproletariat* or (ii) in bourgeois mythology. Two other reviewers noted that Thompson concentrated his attention on 'the desperate fringe of wage earners and petty manufacturers who were being left behind by the march of machinery' and was ignoring the factory proletariat, the miners, building trades, engineers and transport workers. Foster put the spinners back in the picture, but it was not surprising that, in the formative period of working-class consciousness, those whose experience of capitalist competition and change was especially degrading should have taken the lead in trying to understand and combat what was happening to them. No one will ever find a point in history at which the whole of the working class got out of bed one morning with a total awareness of their own identity (although the days after Peterloo with mass meetings in many parts of the country must have come very near this). Dinwiddy quotes the Yorkshire magistrates on the *Black Lamp*: 'the mischief was not extensive . . . ' (*Past and Present*, 1974); and Thomis [1969 and 1970] takes care to isolate Brandreth and the men of the Pentrich rising and the Luddite activists from the bulk of the working population. Frame breaking, he says, was the work of small groups of young men. Modern understanding of guerrilla activity would expect action of this kind to be taken by just such a group, but would see the ability of these men to escape justice as a 'fish and water' problem. The fish could only escape if the rest of the population (the water) was basically sympathetic to what they were doing.[8] The working-class communities in which the Luddites lived were especially opaque and gave little away to the authorities.

The second line of attack has been labelled 'compartmentalist' [Donnelly, 1976]. In some of its aspects it is better called reductionist, especially in the writing of Musson, its most forceful exponent. Musson took the revolutionary activities of Foster's Oldham and reduced each to trades-union activity: wages and hours. He showed that even Doherty and the National Regeneration Society collaborated with middle-class radicals (*Social History*, 1976). Foster used Home Office papers and the speeches of strike leaders to show that Doherty and his fellows envisaged revolutionary change and that the government feared them as leaders of a dangerous movement. It is clear from the evidence that

44

these leaders used conflict and consensus language according to circumstance. We do not yet have the knowledge or the clarity and openness of ideological discussion to decide if Musson's evidence should be dismissed as tactical evasion by revolutionary leaders, or if Foster's evidence should be dismissed as the rhetoric of political and industrial leaders. Thomis with the Luddites and Dinwiddy with the croppers and political activists in Yorkshire in the early 1800s were both anxious to separate the trades-union and the political action which happened at the same time in Yorkshire, Lancashire and Nottinghamshire. Donnelly and Baxter (*Past and Present*, No. 64, 1974) have produced considerable evidence to refute this. It does seem unlikely, in the close-knit working-class communities of those areas, that bitter industrial experience and the political scheming of the Painites could have remained apart for long.

The third line of attack on the Thompson—Foster—Hollis view of class emphasises the lack of homogeneity and unity of purpose amongst the working and middle classes, in terms both of economic fortune and of political action. Pelling [1963] described divisions between labourers and craftsmen and, like Musson [1972], the sectionalism of many occupational groups. Church and Chapman [1967] were sure that the framework knitters acted for themselves as an occupational group with little reference to a working class. J. R. Vincent [1967] in his study of voting habits showed that political behaviour cut across occupational groups, although Neale explained some of the differences within occupations by different levels of property ownership, indicated by rate books. But as Brian Harrison wrote in a review of Neale, the whole point of class feeling is that it cuts across sectional feeling, and unites people despite the differences between them (*New Society*, 2 Nov 1972).

No answer to questions about class consciousness and class relationships can be given with the absolute consistency demanded by these objections. Class is a summary of countless day-to-day experiences, not all of which involve the expression of aggressive sentiments of identity and conflict. The people of Nottinghamshire did not all go around smashing machines, but they saw to it that the boys who did were not caught. Trades-union leaders were not averse to joining in a petition with the small manufacturer or sitting on a platform with a helpful Anglican parson, but this did not necessarily stop them stoning blacklegs in a strike or sharpening pikes when all else failed.

The reader must decide which of the many types of social action discussed in the last few pages were most important for the development of British social relationships in the nineteenth century.

7   On the Influences of Economic Change

MOST historians relate these changes in social relationships and consciousness to changes in economic structure and circumstances. There are three causal models implicit in the literature.

In the first, long-run structural change had a permanently disruptive and destabilising effect, and short-run crises in employment and food supply acted only as the trigger for class action and reaction. The total disruption of social and economic relationships resulted from long-term changes in the institutions of property and the relationships of production: enclosure of land, the concentration of capital and landownership, the end of apprenticeship and wage regulation, and the slow elimination of the independence of the producer. The industrial revolution was for E. P. Thompson 'violence done to human nature', and class was one response to this [Saville, 1969; Foster, 1974; Hobsbawm, 1962; E. P. Thompson, 1963]. Marxist historians are not the only ones to use such a model. Asa Briggs has used the comparative local study to show that class consciousness and hostile class relationships were related to the large units of production in the Lancashire cotton industry, and more conciliatory relationships to the small workshops of Birmingham. The local study allowed a detailed examination of the specific links between economic structure and changes in class consciousness and class action, a task which can only be done very generally at national level.

The second model still concentrated on long-run change but was more concerned with the long-run availability of economic factors, especially food and population. Thus in Chambers's account of rural–urban migration, it is the growth of population which forced people to move into the towns and not the reorganisation of agricultural production centred on enclosure and larger farms (*EcHR*, 1953). In Bythell's (1969) account of the hand-loom weavers it was the increased supply of labour, itself related to population increase, which was the basis of distress rather than the employers' exploitation or the willingness to allow the labour market to be subjected to unrestrained competition. In Perkin's account it was the increase in the size and concentration (urbanisation) of the population which was a major causal factor rather than human action in reorganising economic relationships.

The third causal pattern considered that long-run change was too gradual to have an effect and concentrated on short-run crises in food supply and unemployment. Rostow produced a social tension chart based on trade-cycle patterns and food prices. The results accorded well with observed conflicts from Luddism to the Chartists of 1848, but were much derided by E. P. Thompson for their partial account of what was happening. A recent study of the pan-European subsistence crisis of 1816—17 relates the events of those years, including the Blanketeers and the Pentrich rising, not to radicalism but to food shortages.[9] Corn prices have been related to the politics of the 1840s and the agitation leading up to the Second Reform Act [Kitson Clark, 1953; Vincent, 1966: *268*].

Most historians accept such crises as a spur to political action. In 1836 Attwood wryly quoted Cobbett's warning to political activists, 'I defy you to agitate a fellow on a full stomach.' Grumbling about food shortages and unemployment frequently grew into political action, as with the Sheffield Corresponding Society which began with 'five or six mechanics . . . conversing about the enormous high price of provisions' (quoted by G. A. Williams [1968: *58*]). Such responses can be understood only in terms of wider structural change, unless they are to appear as only temporary deviations from an otherwise stable situation. Hobsbawm identified the problem [1964]. Social movements in Europe developed unevenly in 'leaps' which were closely related in their short-run timing to crises in food prices and employment, but such factors cannot account for the difference in the nature and magnitude of reaction to each crisis. In the 1740s it was the bread riot, in the 1790s Painite conspiracies and in 1839 and 1842—4 Chartism and the trades unions. Why should the change in the content of the response have taken place? The answer can be found only in the tensions created by long-run change.

What happened to economic relationships in the few decades after 1790 did not create class society. That happened slowly over two or three hundred years. What happened was the creation of economic conditions in which the relationships of commercial and capitalist production could no longer remain stable. Let us examine how this result was gained for four very different but important sections of the labour force.

Agricultural labourers were important not only because they

48

formed the largest portion of the labour force but also because they and the peasant small-holding families from which they came were the source of the urban wage labour force essential to industrial growth. Few of those who took part in the mass movements of the industrial revolution were more than one generation away from the countryside. For Maurice Dobb, as for Marx, enclosure and the destruction of the last remaining customary rights (common grazing, game and fuel gathering) played a major part in forcing the future industrial proletariat into the towns. Thorold Rogers claimed this was 'a conspiracy concocted by the law and carried out by the parties interested in its success'.[10] Chambers's demographic work suggested that nothing so simple had occurred (*EcHR*, 1953). Population in enclosed villages increased in the late eighteenth century because the improved efficiency of agriculture created an increased demand for labour. Those who drifted to the towns were the extra people created by the population increase which dated from between 1760 and 1780. The destruction of the English peasantry, which unlike elsewhere in Europe took place before industrialisation, had been a slow process which accelerated in the late seventeenth century. By 1831 well over 75 per cent of the population in agriculture was part of a wage labour–capital relationship.

During the eighteenth century agriculture was fully commercialised. Actions were dominated by cash transactions and the profit motive, not by customary relationships [Saville, 1969]. Old rights to fuel, game and grazing were drawn into the cash economy. Legal arrangements ranging from the limitations on entail to the game laws increased the pressures of the cash economy. Population increase may not have been part of a conspiracy; but given the structure of law and property ownership, the surplus population had no choice but to move into the towns. Under a different economic structure the sub-division of peasant holdings might have been an alternative, though not an attractive one given the examples of Ireland and Highland Scotland. Recent work has provided new evidence for the old belief that the increase in population was stimulated by the creation of a wage labour force which was prepared to marry early as there was no longer any point in delaying marriage until a smallholding was available.[11] The increasing segregation within rural society was marked not only by the decline of the smallholder but also by the social segregation of the capitalist tenant farmer from his labour force, symbolised by the decline of the practice of master and unmarried farm servants dining together at the farm table [Perkin, 1969:*147*]. The agricultural labourer was the victim of change. His response was mainly traditional, as in the threshing-machine-smashing Swing riots of 1831 [Hobsbawm and Rudé, 1969]. The agricultural labourer took little part in the newer means of class assertion (trades unionism and Chartism), although the incident of the Tolpuddle labourers transported for forming a union suggested that structural weakness (being scattered in different farms and threatened by unemployment and the New Poor Law) was the cause, rather than any lack of will or class consciousness.

The increase in factory production in cotton and the other textile industries dominated the discussion of economic change in this period. Perkin, quoting Engels, pointed out that class formation was not based on the factory as such but on the concentration of factories in the towns which took place with the change from water to steam power after 1780–1800 [Perkin, 1969: *178–9*]. Studies of the Manchester area have related the bitter class divisions of the 1832 reform agitation and the aggressive class-conscious nature of Chartism to the clear-cut class divisions and hostility produced by the factory [Briggs, 1950–2; Read, in Briggs, 1959(b)]. The concentration of capital and the polarisation of society caused by the technological base of the factory should not be exaggerated. Despite the activities of giants like the Peels in Lancashire and David Dale at New Lanark, the small firm retained a major place in the textile industry. Indeed after 1830 and the end of the era of abnormal profits, the giants failed to make further inroads into the industry.[12]

The factory was associated with several innovations in class behaviour. The cotton spinners provided only background support for the democratic radicals of the 1790s and 1815–20, but they played a major part in the development of industrial trades unions. The spinners had a tradition of sectional and community-based trades clubs, often taking the form of friendly societies, which formed loose affiliations for assisting those tramping for work, for resisting wage reductions and the introduction of machinery. In the factory the spinners quickly developed a tradition of militant labour organisation. The years up to 1830 saw a series of cotton spinners' unions. Their power was regional, based on Lancashire, and their success sporadic and temporary [Turner,

1962]. Led by John Doherty, the spinners made several attempts to organise labour on a general and national basis, culminating in the Grand National Consolidated Trades Union of 1834. These had only brief success and existence: problems of organisation and gaining mass support could not be solved by men who were only part way to understanding the threats to their living-standards and independence at work [Cole, 1953; Turner, 1962].

More substantial in their achievement were the regionally based industrial unions whose ambitions arose out of the practical needs of trades disputes in the setting of factory and national and international markets. The concentration of labour in the mills made it easier for those involved to perceive their common situation, and thus become more easily convinced of the need for combination. Practical problems like the collection of subscriptions and the spreading of information were easier than in scattered farming and handworking communities. The mill was easier to picket than scattered workshops. Blacklegs were met with a mixture of violence and persuasion. They were as likely to have their fares paid to go home as to be met with a half brick and shouts of 'nobstick'. The need to counter blacklegging turned the thoughts of Doherty and other leaders to the need for national and general unions. The strikes were still regional and men could be recruited in other regions, often in ignorance of their strike-breaking function. With most factory occupations outsiders could be trained to a fair degree of proficiency in a short period of time to provide an alternative labour force. Thus national and general unions were essential to organise this large potential labour market. In light of such practical needs and the experience of uncontrolled competition, the union activists were naturally attracted to the new class ideologies of the 1830s which promised a radical transformation of society [Cole, 1953]. At a practical level, the success of these unions was a reflection of the short-run market position of labour. In the long run their achievement was the slow creation of a wide range of political ambitions amongst the labour force.

Factory employment created a new set of working-class political ambitions centred on the demand for legislative control of hours and conditions in the factory. The Short-Time Committees of Lancashire and Yorkshire had little use for the old demand for apprenticeship and wage regulations, but fought a propaganda and political battle for better factory acts, and above all for the limitation of labour to ten hours per day. Foster [1974] believed that this issue was the one which linked economic and political affairs in the minds of the Oldham operatives, and thus made their consciousness distinct from that of the seamen of South Shields and the shoemakers of Northampton. The cotton masters likewise were central to the creation of middle-class political ambitions; first through their demand for the vote in 1832, and more important through the campaign for the repeal of the Corn Laws in 1838–46. They demanded repeal not as an interest group but as the representatives of a class. The impact of the Corn Laws and their repeal on British prices and output is still a matter for debate[13] but that repeal was essential as a symbol of aristocratic government's responsiveness to middle-class power [Kemp, 1961]. Support for the Anti-Corn Law League was patchy, temporary, and largely based on Manchester. What was new in the history of class relationships was the manner in which the League saw itself and was seen by its opponents as 'the middle class' [Briggs, 1959(a); McCord, 1958 and 1967].

Factory production affected a minority of the labour force and a small portion of the national product, but because it represented, in an extreme form, changes taking place in other sections of the economy, and because it represented the dominant future form of workplace relationships, the factory was of central importance to the development of class.

The increase in the intensity of work which took place after 1780 was nowhere clearer than in the factory. Pollard [1965] has shown that the new manufacturers faced many problems of discipline and management. The labour force, used to the easier routine of domestic and workshop industry, had to meet exacting standards of accuracy, regularity and order in their work so that the whole factory might be co-ordinated with the water wheel or the steam engine. Most employers coerced their employees with fines and the threat of dismissal. Others provided housing, places of worship and schools, and encouraged insurance schemes. Some did this perforce because of the isolated nature of their mill sites; some because they saw such action as an opportunity for the paternalistic control of their labour force. Throughout the economy there was a wholesale replacement of the natural work rhythms of the seasons and the domestic craftsman by the time discipline of the mill clock and the foreman's fob watch [E. P. Thompson, 1967]. Symptomatic of this was the steady reduction in the number of bank holidays over the period, and the attacks on traditional leisure activities, so that by the 1840s only chapel and public house filled the gloomy gap between bearbaiting and the maypole on one hand and association football and the music hall on the other [B. H. Harrison, 1967].

The writing on the hand-loom weavers shows agreement on the course of economic change but very different conclusions about that group's contribution to class consciousness [Bythell, 1969; E. P. Thompson, 1963]. The weavers' wage rates declined from a peak in the mid-1790s. They may have compensated for this fall by working longer hours, for many accounts of the weavers in this period talk of lost leisure time. The initial decline was brought about not by the power loom, which was introduced by Cartwright in 1785, but by a large labour surplus. The trade was easy to learn and the growing population provided many recruits, some of whom used weaving as a casual trade to supplement income from agriculture or other trades like shoemaking and joinery. The frequent trade slumps caused by the dislocations of war in international trade were the occasion for the reductions in wages. Foster saw these as deliberate attacks by the masters on the living-standards of the workers (see above, p. 40). For Bythell the decline was the result of market forces, especially the rise in labour supply, and after 1826 the extensive introduction of the power loom which, after many improvements upon Cartwright's economically fairly useless innovation, had become profitable.

The weavers responded to this decline in four different ways. Trades-union action was difficult in such a large and scattered labour force. Success was possible for specialised groups like the Bolton counterpane weavers, but the general weavers' unions were more fragile. Wage gains were made in 1808 on the peak of a trade boom, but in 1818 increased labour supply created the conditions for failure. The weavers (like the framework knitters) turned to parliament for help with frequent petitions for legislation to enforce minimum wages; parliament just as frequently refused to act.

The weavers were among several groups who looked to the eighteenth-century paternalistic system of wage and apprenticeship regulation as a solution to the problems caused by their weak market position. The operation of market forces was a major influence on the class experience of all occupational groups, but with the exception of Bythell's study this influence has rarely been fully analysed. It must be remembered that these market forces were allowed to operate by what Thomas Carlyle called the 'abdication on the part of the governors' [Perkin, 1969: *182*]. Most important was the manner in which wage and apprenticeship regulations were first allowed to fall into disuse and then repealed in the early years of the century [E. P. Thompson, 1963: *517*]. Indeed a major part of class struggle consists of attempts to alter the terms and conditions within which market forces operate: legislation and trades-union action are the clearest examples of this. The weavers turned with mounting violence to a third traditional tactic – smashing machinery. The breaking of the power looms culminated in a major attack on the factories in the slump of 1826, but once the power loom had become economically viable in the 1830s, such violence was no deterrent to the masters.

Last of all the weavers turned to radical politics. They took some part in the Hampden clubs of 1817 and, after the failure of their strike in 1818, turned vigorous attention to the agitation of 1819. Out of the 200 on the books of the Metropolitan Relief Committee, which sent aid to the victims of Peterloo, 150 were weavers. In 1838 the weavers turned up again as Chartists. For Thompson the experience of the weavers was a major contribution to working-class formation, especially the sense of loss of economic reward and the failure to gain any help from parliament. Bythell was concerned with the lack of continuity in the weavers' radical political activities; 'political radicalism [was] a lowest common denominator which all workers might seize upon when some temporary setback seemed particularly severe' [Bythell, 1969: *217*].

Relevant here is Foster's division of the working population into the mass whose temporary activity needed sustaining by experience and education, and those whose leadership provided continuity and who made continuous attempts to understand what was happening and to develop ideological and organisational skills from their experience. Also relevant was the manner in which other groups among the working population, not least the cotton spinners, saw the weavers' decline as a warning. The weavers among the blacklegs in the 1829 spinners' strike were evidence of a lack of working-class solidarity. It was also a lesson in the need for a wider working-class consciousness than that provided by the sectionalism of the industrial unions. The politics and general unions of the 1830s attempted to use this lesson. Bythell was correct when he said that there was no necessary link between extreme poverty and radicalism. Foster also showed that his most radical town, Oldham, had less poverty than Northampton or South Shields. The crucial feature of the weavers' experience was not their poverty, which was extreme, but the memories of a former comfortable status. Thwarted expectations of just economic reward were and are a major factor in class action.

The London artisan was central to the history of radical politics, inheriting eighteenth-century and Painite traditions and developing a critique of capitalist economic relationships through Owenism and later socialism, but above all through Chartism. The moderately paid members of the artisan class were the backbone of Chartism [Prothero, 1969]. The benefits of industrialisation may well have reached the artisan first [Perkin, 1969: *144*]. The 30-shillings-a-week artisan — the engineer and the millwright as well as many in traditional crafts — had better housing, a better diet and a richer cultural life of libraries, institutes and chapels. They were able to sustain trade societies to protect that standard of living. Their position was far superior to the mill operative who might bring home 15s. to 20s. a week when in full work. The artisan gained and retained his economic status not only by the fortune of the market, in which skilled labour was in short supply, but also by organisation: the defence of workshop routine, the control of apprenticeship to limit entry to the trade, and the refusal to work with men who had not served their time.

The end of apprenticeship regulations in 1813, the increase in the supply of labour as population rose, the opportunities provided by trade slump and the seasonality of demand, and above all the reorganisation of work to reduce the amount of skilled labour needed, meant that an increasing number of trades lost their artisan status, or saw the work divided between the honorable 'society' men, where the craft societies kept control, and the dishonourable trades, controlled by the subcontractors, garret masters and sweaters who produced cheap ready-made 'slop' furniture and clothing. These changes created an awareness of the importance of political action, hence the artisan support for Chartism [E. P. Thompson, 1963; Hollis, 1973]. The artisans were another group whose class consciousness was aroused by the thwarting of just expectations by economic change.

The influence of commercial relationships on artisan production extended rapidly in the 1840s. Once the power of the craft societies had been broken the 'Mayhew' effect rapidly reduced earnings. In his massive enquiries into London labour in mid-century, Mayhew found that once wages began to fall, then individuals would work longer hours to try and maintain their earnings, thus increasing the supply of labour, and providing further opportunities for wage cutting [Thompson and Yeo, 1971; Stedman Jones, 1971: *ch. 4*]. Pelling [1963] found that many industries were untouched by steam and machine for much of the nineteenth century. This was true but did not protect the labour force of such industries from changes in workplace relationships and in the intensity of labour. The industrial revolution was a matter not only of steam and technological change but also of Adam Smith and his pins — that is, of the increasing sub-division and reorganisation of labour to increase productivity and reduce costs (*Wealth of Nations*, 1776, ch. 1, 'Of the Division of Labour').

8   On Maintaining Social Authority

WE have described conditions of inequality and exploitation which changed in their nature and intensity. The discussion of class consciousness showed that such conditions were being increasingly questioned. In this situation the problem of maintaining order and social authority became acute. The means by which that authority was maintained changed during the industrial revolution. Main force, a militia and the occasional use of regular troops always had a place in keeping order in the eighteenth century. At the first shock of Jacobinism and rising radical and trades-union action, the ruling class intensified their use of main force. In 1794 the Volunteers were raised, partly to counter the threat of French invasion and partly to use for internal security. The Volunteers were mainly gentry, tenant farmers, shopkeepers, professional men and the 'employers on horseback' [Western, 1956]. After Peterloo the use of the Volunteers decreased as the authorities realised that the presence of the yeomanry exacerbated class feeling rather than restoring social peace. Regular troops were essential throughout the Chartist period and beyond. Indeed the most violent Chartist years of 1839 and 1840 were noted for the skill with which the authorities deployed their forces. General Sir Charles James Napier restrained the desire of the local magistrates for strong measures and followed a policy of using a judicious show of force, and then adopting a low profile during the mass meetings, often meeting with Chartist leaders to ensure that troops and people never came into conflict. Meanwhile the Home Office was directing a carefully planned campaign of arresting Chartist leaders, most of whom were committed for two- or three-year terms of imprisonment, effectively breaking up the coherence of the movement at local level.

The most important change in the period was the introduction of a bureaucratically organised police force, which established a strong and regular presence in working-class areas, first in London in 1829, then in the municipal towns after 1836 and in the counties after 1839. Their introduction was bitterly resisted by many working-class communities and their radical and trades-union leaders. The 'blue bottles' were comfortably dressed and paid 18s. a week to walk around doing nothing except interfere with the activities of working people; political meetings were dispersed (especially if they were held on Sunday), strike breakers escorted to work and street traders moved on. The London coster had a special hatred of the police. Countless leisure activities like drinking, footracing, dog fighting and street gambling were harassed. In the north of England the new police were greeted by serious riots, especially in areas where physical force Chartism and anti-Poor Law feeling were strong. By the 1850s the police had, like the trades unions, gained wider acceptance (though rarely popularity) amongst their class opponents [Storch, 1975; Midwinter, 1968].

Few systems of social authority can rely on main force alone for long. In recent years historians have paid increasing attention to the concept of hegemony and related ideas. This is a far-reaching and complex idea developed from the ideas of Marx and Lenin by the Italian communist Gramsci [1971]. The bulk of his writing was done in prison, and what emerged was a continuous parable of the manner in which those in authority maintain their power.

> By 'hegemony' Gramsci seems to mean a socio-political situation, in his terminology a 'moment' in which the philosophy and practice of a society fuse or are in equilibrium; an order in which a certain way of life and thought is dominant, in which one concept of reality is diffused throughout society in all its institutional and private manifestations, informing with its spirit all taste, morality, customs, religious and political principles, and all social relationships, particularly in their intellectual and moral connotations. An element of direction and control, not necessarily conscious, is implied. (From Gwyn Williams, in *Journal of the History of Ideas*, 1960.)

In nineteenth-century Britain, as in nineteenth- and twentieth-century Italy of which Gramsci wrote so much, two socio-political groupings were involved in hegemonic activity. First there were those who controlled the state and sought to maintain the stability of the state, and then there were those sections of the middle class who aspired to gain a dominant and controlling position within British society for their own social class. As such an effort also involved maintaining social stability, there was co-operation as well as tension between the ideas and actions of these two groups. It is within this framework of analysis that Perkin's discussion of the struggle of ideals might be developed.

In Britain the so-called 'spontaneous consent', through which those who were ruled acquiesced in the power exercised over them by the rulers, had been gained traditionally through religion and education. The anxieties of the 1790s brought an intensification of religious and educational activity by the middle and ruling classes: Sunday Schools, religious revivals, Bible and Tract Societies and a host of other activities associated with the evangelical revival. This began as an attack on the lax morals and the religious apathy of upper and working classes by an upper-middle-class group of Anglicans and Nonconformists, but the middle classes rapidly saw the value of religious enthusiasm for law and order. In 1797 Wilberforce wrote that the church 'renders the inequalities of the social state less galling to the lower orders, whom she also instructs in their turn to be diligent, humble and patient' (*Practical View of the Prevailing Religious System of Professed Christians in the Higher and Middle Classes* . . . , quoted by Kiernan [1952]). It would be wrong to see this as a conspiracy. Men like Wilberforce had a genuine concern for the immortal souls of those they addressed. None the less, these activities had a considerable impact on social relationships, perhaps more on the ruling classes, motivating and legitimising ideological preaching.

Throughout the period the middle and upper classes placed more and more value on education as social discipline. The link between Sunday Schools and primary education and the order and discipline of the labour force was realised early [Simon, 1960]. The Mechanics Institutions were promoted from the mid-1820s by those like Dr Williamson, the Leeds physician, who said, 'Political events had given an unusual excitement to the thinking powers of the great mass of society [it was 1832], the right direction of which depends chiefly on the adoption of an extensive system of instruction' (*Leeds Mercury*, 22 Sep 1832). J. F. C. Harrison [1961] described the Mechanics Institutions and the growing literature of self-help and useful knowledge, like *Chambers' Edinburgh Journal* and the *Penny Magazine*, as an attempt by the middle classes to make the working classes in their own image (see also R. K. Webb [1955]). In the 1840s James Kay Shuttleworth (the same Dr Kay who had written about Manchester in 1832) used his ten difficult years as secretary to the Committee of the Privy Council on Education to ensure a place in government policy for an efficient system of national primary education which would maintain social authority. He emphasised the 'civilising' mission of schools and schoolteachers upon the misguided behaviour and thoughts of the working classes [Johnson, 1970].

Hegemonic activity involves more than ideological propaganda. It involves the control of ideas and the means of communicating ideas and information to ensure that the ideas, information and values in mass circulation will support the legitimacy of the authority of the ruling classes, and that the information about social organisations and relationships which is available will make the acceptance of that dominant value system much easier. If hegemonic control became absolute then it would be impossible for subordinate groups to envisage and develop any system of knowledge except that which legitimated the existing power structure. Did this happen in Britain between 1790 and 1850? Certainly the period saw increasing middle-class efforts to influence working-class culture and values. These efforts intensified from the 1820s onwards. Mechanics Institutions, Temperance Societies and Savings Banks were all part of a middle-class voluntary effort designed to transform working-class behaviour and ideals, an effort which Foster calls 'cultural aggression'. Foster saw a well calculated series of concessions, notably the repeal of the Combination Acts in 1825 and the Ten Hours Act of 1847, as designed to divide working-class political leadership and convince working people that their real needs and interests could be served by the existing social system. Close examination of all these movements shows a complex of motives – guilt, humanitarianism, religious feeling – in addition to a well calculated and enlightened self-interest.

Was all this effort successful? The working classes were not as helpless in the grip of hegemonic power as the theory might suggest. The newspaper stamp duty was a deliberate attempt to price news and analysis out of the pocket of working people. From 1830 onwards a variety of radical journalists like Hetherington and Doherty deliberately broke the law, suffering police raids, fines and imprisonment in a campaign which not only created an alternative press circulating information and ideas unfavourable to the ruling class, but also led to the repeal of all but the last penny of the newspaper tax in 1836 [Hollis, 1970]. The main evidence for the success of middle-class cultural domination was provided by the key place of the artisan in the social peace of the 1850s. His trades unions were unable to negotiate in any terms but those of political economy, and their values of respectability, respect for saving, education and family life, and above all their abandonment of the leadership of the working classes through movements like Chartism all support this case. It has not yet been resolved how far artisan culture in the 1850s was dominated by a middle-class cultural conspiracy and how far it was a thriving independent culture which coincided with middle-class values at many points but which selected from the values and organisations offered by the middle and ruling classes only those that suited artisan interests [Clements, 1961; Gray, 1976; Crossick, 1976].

9   Class, Status and Party

THE bulk of the history of class has been written by the Marxist, neo-Marxist and anti-Marxist. Thus the whole shape of the discussion of class in the industrial revolution – the concepts used and the questions asked – has been derived from Marx. Most of the present book, of necessity, follows the working out of these questions in an ample literature.

Weber provided an alternative system by which historians can organise the information they have about class relationships in the past. It is a pity that his ideas have been so little used by historians. This section sketches the manner in which a student might use Weberian ideas. In his discussion of class, status and party Weber identified three aspects or dimensions of the distribution of power in society, three types of social group with which men could identify themselves and justify their behaviour and fortunes.

An individual's economic class was determined by his market situation, which in turn depended on the value of his labour and his share of property. In theory such a definition would create an infinite number of classes, as each individual had a slightly different market position. In practice the class situations of many people clustered together to form the major class groupings in society. Weber found four in late nineteenth-century Europe: (i) the manual working class which he divided into skilled and unskilled; (ii) the petty bourgeoisie; (iii) the propertyless white-collar workers; and (iv) those privileged through property and education [Gerth and Mills, 1948; Giddens, 1973: 48]. Economic class was implicit in everyone's market situation and had a major influence on his life chances.

Weber recognised that an economic class could be a basis for a sense of community and conflict, but held that such a development was not necessary. Individuals identified themselves with status groups which were the basis of a consciousness of common interests and values. Each individual and group was placed according to the degree of 'social honour' accorded them by the rest of society. Society was stratified into a series of status groups distinguished by common life styles and social evaluation. The boundaries of these groups were often marked by inter-marrying and inter-dining limits. Whilst the possibility of making successful claims for status often depended on income and wealth, other factors such as race, religion and occupation were equally important.

Party was the organisation through which an individual and those like him laid claim to power in an organised way.

The Marxist would naturally expect the social groups identified by the application of these three concepts to converge. Thus status and consciousness would derive from economic class and organised party action from both. Weber presented no linear scheme of the development of industrial society. He expected economic class divisions would become more important than any other and that wages rather than credit or the price of bread would become the major issue between classes. He dismissed the claim that industrial capitalism would bring about the absolute or relative deprivation of the worker, or that industrial society would polarise into two great social classes. Instead he saw a tendency to a plurality of social classes with a diverse set of class relationships. Class, status and party provided three competing systems of social organisation which were unlikely to converge. Finally he saw the growth of bureaucracy, not as the agent of ruling-class domination, but as the agency which ensured the rational use and development of resources, technology and social relationships (including those of domination) [Giddens, 1973: 46; Gerth and Mills, 1948: 196]. The use of Weberian concepts need not commit the historian to Weber's account of the nineteenth century, but their use encompasses a wider range of evidence and possibilities without precluding the Marxist outcome to any analysis.

Little can be added here to what has already been said about economic class and the market position of different groups in society. Two points need to be emphasised: first the enormous variation of earnings within all social classes, especially the working class; and second the importance of regularity of earnings in determining the economic fortunes of individual members of that class. In general high wages and regularity of work went together. In one West Riding survey done in 1839, the cloth-drawers topped the list with 24s. 6d. per week and twelve months full work, whilst the weavers, shoemakers and woolcombers collected 13s. to 14s. per week and only had ten months work in an average year. Only the outdoor building workers had more irregular work. The difference between economic class and status is best illustrated by the mechanics and clerks:

Although comparatively high wages may be earned by this class [the mechanics], the effect of their miserable economy is more strikingly marked by a comparison of the conditions of persons in other classes: such for instance as merchants' or lawyers' clerks with salaries from £70 to £80 per year, with the conditions of mechanics earning from 30s. to £2 per week. The one will be comparatively well fed, well lodged and respectable in appearance; whilst the other lives in a hovel; his wife perhaps is seen filthy and idle, and his children about the streets, without a shoe to their foot or a decent rag to cover them. (From *The Educational Magazine and Journal of Christian Philanthropy and Public Utility*, 1835.)

Historians talk a great deal about status. Status ambitions play an important part in explaining the motivation for middle- and sometimes skilled working-class behaviour. Perkin saw striving for status as the driving force behind entrepreneurial ambition during the industrial revolution. The seeking for the 'social prestige and power over neighbours that went with property', not just the possession of property itself, was what drove men to take commercial and manufacturing risks [Perkin, 1969: *85*]. The evaluation of status was not a simple matter. Perkin showed that the late eighteenth century saw a competition between birth and property as evaluators of status, and that the status attributed to the younger sons of the aristocracy was amply justified by their access to patronage through their families. There was nothing empty about status. It always had a sound practical basis, however much that basis might be hidden. The status attributed to land had a solid economic base. As Richard Crawshay, the ironmaster, wrote, 'nothing but land can be considered as safe.' No one was better placed than the nineteenth-century novelist to show the complexities of competing status systems. The tensions and anxieties of marriage and courtship across status barriers was a major theme of the novels of the 1840s [Tillotson, 1954]. The 'silver fork' novels and etiquette manuals of the years before 1850 demonstrated middle-class curiosity about and desire to emulate the life style and manners of the aristocracy which the Anti-Corn Law League was teaching them to despise. One example from Mrs Gaskell's *North and South* must serve. Margaret Hale, the well-bred parson's daughter, left the south of England with a contempt for 'the pretence that makes the vulgarity of shop people' and for 'the gambling spirit of trade'. She meets the Manchester manufacturer, Mr Thornton, with his pride in the mill and the capital built up by his skill, hard work and hard bargaining: 'I would rather be a man toiling and suffering — nay, failing and successless — here, than lead a dull prosperous life in the old worn grooves of what you call more aristocratic society down in the south, with their slow days of careless ease.' The novel ends with the two married, a perfect allegory of the merging of the two status systems in the 1850s. As yet historians have produced few studies of status-related behaviour, apart from the marriage studies by Foster and Gray. Leonore Davidoff has shown the manner in which the etiquette and the 'season' which dominated upper-class social life from the middle of the century provided a status-related means of filtering those who wished to enter the society of those with power, whether as marriage partners or as dinner guests.

Status has so far been considered as an influence on small groupings (the inter-dining and inter-marrying groups), but after 1850 Britain developed two status concepts of a very different kind: those of 'the gentleman' and of 'respectability'. These created a means of evaluation across a wide range of the smaller status groups, making it possible for men of different social backgrounds to co-operate together in politics and public affairs. A gentleman had the assurance and leisure which wealth brought. He was judged by moral standards of selflessness, courage, independence and self-control. Above all a gentleman was marked by his acceptance as a member of the élite. But which élite? Those who dined comfortably with the leaders of Leeds or Birmingham often had no chance of reaching the balls and receptions of the London season. This made the idea of a gentleman so indefinite and so powerful. Being a gentleman imposed a code of behaviour, but this might vary with different élites. One would demand a subscription to the local hospital, whilst another, dominated by the Jockey Club, required that a man pay his gambling debts without question [Best, 1971: 254]. The idea of a gentleman could cross barriers of wealth and even class, gently uniting aristocratic birth with landed wealth, industrial wealth and professional prestige.

Respectability had even greater power. The claim to respectability was made through a style of life. Living within one's means and financial independence were crucial; hence it was easier to be respectable on £500 than on £50 a year. Habits of frugality, saving, sobriety – even teetotalism – were important, as were clean and tidy clothes and houses. Education, religion, rigid sexual propriety and family-centred values and social life all marked a life style which sought to assert order and self-control on the lives of individuals faced with the uncertainties of industrial society. This life style is frequently called middle-class.

The middle class had no monopoly of respectability. Some imitated the middle class to gain recognition for a clerk's job, a schoolteaching post or even a dole from the local church coal and clothing fund. But from the beginning of the century others had used 'respectability' as part of a powerful claim for civil and political rights. Sobriety, family values and a respect for education were prominent among the radical groups of the French War period [E. P. Thompson, 1963: *740*]. William Lovett felt that sobriety was as much part of the working-class claim for the vote as the Chartist threats. Middle-class leaders, like the whig newspaper editor Edward Baines, did indeed reject working-class claims for the franchise because he saw an illiterate, drunken and disorderly class unfit to exercise the vote. Such pessimism was unwarranted. There were few friendly societies and trades clubs which did not include rules against persistent drunkenness, swearing and disorderly conduct. There was some evidence, notably the manner in which Gladstone declared himself impressed by working-class savings habits, that the respectability of the artisan made it easier for those with power to grant an extension of the franchise in 1867. The ideas of the gentleman and respectability could justify detailed stratification and inequality. They could also help the mutual acceptability and co-operation of unequal social groups in politics and public affairs.

Party was the means by which men organised themselves in their search for power. Much has already been said about the ruling class and the working classes. The former organised through the state and the leadership of the major political parties, and the latter through the rise and fall of networks of political clubs and trades unions. Their growing ability to organise in a formal manner was a distinctive feature of the period: 'the poor when suffering and dissatisfied no longer make a riot but hold a meeting . . . ' (Manchester, 1819, quoted by E. P. Thompson [1963: *424*]. After

1850 the use of formal organisation by working people was increasingly accepted by the middle and ruling classes [Briggs, 1959(a): *410*; Perkin, 1969: *340–407*]. The middle class had no permanent organisation with which to identify. The aristocracy retained their control of the state after 1832 by a mixture of power and a willingness to meet minimal middle-class demands for change. The middle class continued, as before 1832, to operate through a series of extra-parliamentary movements and pressure groups. It was a class of movements, each one limited and temporary in its activities, but by their influence, and by their overlapping ideals and membership, they created a formidable presence in British society. Anti-Slavery, Bible Societies , Sunday Schools, protests against Pitt's income tax and against the Orders in Council in 1812, the Reform agitation in 1830–2, the Anti-Corn Law League, the Peace Society and the Administrative Reform Association: these were the major organisations through which a class divergent in its interests and varied in its ideology carried its influence into national life.

Although party was the means by which men organised themselves in their search for power, there is no necessity that such a search should bring together men united by a common social class. Nationalism and religion competed for loyalty with social class. Irish loyalty to O'Connell and the repeal movement diverted many away from Chartism. This was important for working-class formation when Irish-born made up 5 to 10 per cent of the population of the large industrial cities. Little is known of the influence of Scottish and Welsh feeling, though the Scots had their own distinctive type of Chartism, and nationalist feeling among the middle classes was one factor in the Disruption of the Kirk in 1843. For the English, Foster notes that anti-Irish and anti-Russian feeling played a part in weakening the aggressive working-class consciousness of the 1840s.

Even the major political parties had no class identity. At national level they were aristocratic alliances in competition for power. At local level the whig/tory division was nearly the same as the Nonconformist/Anglican division. Briggs [1959(a)] and Perkin [1969] both see religious divisions not as a diversion from class identity but as a prototype of class feeling.

This question has been examined in most detail by those discussing the relationship between Methodism and the working classes. Halévy believed that in the influence of Methodism could be found the key to Britain's escape from political revolution on the French scale. He referred to the influence of Methodism and evangelicalism on ruling-class as well as working-class behaviour. The subsequent literature has paid more attention to the working class. Thompson, like Halévy, saw Methodism as a major diversion of energy from class action, as an alternative means of tackling the problems of a period of rapid social change, and as a curb on the polarising tendencies of industrial society. Others saw Methodism as a training-ground for the world of radical politics and trades unions, and indeed Methodist hymns and imagery figured in the speeches and meetings of radicals and unions, from Peterloo to Chartism and beyond [Perkin, 1969; Hill, 1973: *ch. 9*]. Hobsbawm questioned how far some 150,000 English and Welsh Methodists in 1811 could have influenced the behaviour of 10 million people if revolution had really been a possibility [Hobsbawm, 1964: *23*]. Recent studies have shown that class divisions, and disputes over the proper relationship of one class to another, were a major cause of divisions within Methodism, especially in the splits between the loyalist, tory-inclined Wesleyan church and the radical breakaway groups like the Kilhamite or 'Tom Paine' Methodists and the Primitive Methodists.

*

The period ends with the change from the world of Ebenezer Elliott and Ernest Jones to that of W. S. Gilbert:

> Avenge the plundered poor, O Lord,
> But not with fire, but not with sword,
> Not as at Peterloo they died
> Beneath the hoofs of coward pride.
> (from Elliott's *The Jacobin's Prayer*)

> The factories gave forth lurid fires
> From pent up hells within their breast
>
> . . .
>
> Here are men, and engines yonder,
> I see nothing but machines

While the rich with power unstable
Crushed the pauper's heart in vain,
As though the rich were heirs of Abel
And the poor were sons of Cain;

While the bloated trader passes,
Lord of loom and lord of mill;
On his pathway rush the masses,
Crushed beneath his stubborn will.
                    (from Ernest Jones's *The Factory Town*)

Bow, bow, ye lower middle classes,
Bow, bow, ye tradesmen, bow ye masses;
Blow the trumpets, bang the brasses.
Tantantara. Tzing. Boom.
                    (from Gilbert's *Iolanthe*)

This was the world of the social peace of the 1850s and 1860s, of new model unionism, of peers and capitalists sitting together on the boards of railway companies, and of the Second Reform Act of 1867, admitting the artisan within the pale of the constitution. Despite several great strikes, it was an era with a reputation for social peace which concealed the potential for conflict revealed in the events of the 1880s and 1900s.

The industrial revolution belonged, like political economy and Owenism, to the period ' . . . in which the class struggle was as yet undeveloped' [Marx, *Capital*: 14]. Hence the many uncertainties of the study of class in this period. There are no absolutely correct answers in the study of the history of class. The subject must be written with all the consistency, logic and demands for evidence which history can make. The history of class must be the history of the actual and concrete, and not just of abstractions and theories. The history of class was the history of John Doherty addressing the striking cotton workers with the ideas of Owen buzzing in his head; it was the history of Kay Shuttleworth working himself to a nervous breakdown at the Education Department with the ideas of the evangelicals, of Swiss theorists, and of the political economists as well as the memories of poverty and violence in Manchester in his mind. But in the end historians must take their own values and perceptions to the past so that the study of the history of class remains a relationship between them and the people of the past.

Notes and References

The abbreviation *EcHR* represents *Economic History Review*, second series.

1. Habakkuk, H. J., 'Daniel Finch, Second Earl of Nottingham: His House and Estate', in J. H. Plumb (ed.), *Studies in Social History* (London, 1955).
2. Rudé, G., *Wilkes and Liberty* (Oxford, 1962) pp. 105–48; Wilson, R., *Gentleman Merchants: the Merchant Community in Leeds, 1700–1830* (Manchester, 1971).
3. Hill, C., *Puritanism and Revolution* (London, 1958) ch. 10.
4. See Gosden, P. H. J., *The Friendly Societies in England, 1815–1875* (Manchester, 1960).
5. Hudson, D., *Munby, Man of two Worlds: The Life and Diaries of Arthur J. Munby, 1828–1910* (London, 1972).
6. Walmsley, Robert, *Peterloo: The Case Re-opened* (Manchester, 1969); see also extended review, 'Man Bites Yeoman', *Times Literary Supplement*, 11 December 1969.
7. Yeo, S., 'On the Uses of "Apathy"', *Archives Européennes de Sociologie*, xv (1974).
8. Kitson, F., *Low Intensity Operations, Subversion, Insurgency and Peace-keeping* (London, 1971).
9. Post, J. D., *The Last Great Subsistence Crisis in the Western World* (Baltimore and London, 1977) ch. 3.
10. Dobb, M., *Studies in the Development of Capitalism* (London, 1948) p. 233.
11. Levine, D., 'The Demographic Implications of Rural Industrialization: A Family Re-construction Study of Shepshed, Leicestershire', *Social History*, No. 2 (1976).
12. Chapman, S. D., 'Fixed Capital Formation in the British Cotton Industry', *EcHR*, xxiii (1970); Gatrell, V. A. C., 'Labour, Power and Size of Firms in Lancashire Cotton during the Third Quarter of the Nineteenth Century', *EcHR*, xxx (1977).
13. Fairlie, Susan, 'The Corn Laws and British Wheat Production, 1829–1876', *EcHR*, xxii (1969) produced evidence which suggested that the corn laws maintained British wheat output and a large gap between British prices and European prices, 1815–46.

Select Bibliography

This list is only a tithe of the material I have used: my apologies to authors of other works which I have plundered for ideas and information. Items useful for further bibliographical reference are marked with an asterisk (*). Works are referred to in the text by author's name and date of publication, with page reference if necessary.

EcHR here, as in the text and in the Notes and References, refers to the *Economic History Review*, second series.

SECTION I: MAINLY THEORETICAL

These items I have found helpful in framing questions:

Gerth, H. H., and Mills, C. Wright, *From Max Weber, Essays in Sociology* (London, 1948). Includes extracts on bureaucracy and on class, status and party.

Giddens, Anthony, *Capitalism and Modern Social Theory: An Analysis of the Writing of Marx, Durkheim and Weber* (Cambridge, 1971); and *The Class Structure of Advanced Societies* (London, 1973). Together these form the best critical survey of the major sociological approaches to class.

Gramsci, Antonio, *Selections from Prison Notebooks*, edited and translated by Quintin Hoare and Geoffrey Nowell Smith (London, 1971).

Marshall, T. H., *Citizenship and Social Class* (Cambridge, 1950).

Marx, Karl, *Capital: A Critical Analysis of Capitalist Production* (first published in German in 1867; in English in 1886). Interwoven with the better-known theoretical contribution, vol. 1 contains the earliest academic history of class in Britain. Marx paid special attention to the Factory Acts and the transformation of British agriculture.

Marx, Karl, and Engels, Frederick, *The German Ideology* (1846). A compact exposition of historical materialism, with an abstract of the social and economic development of Western capitalism, this is the best introduction to Marx for the historian; skip the polemical bits.

Best, G., *Mid-Victorian Britain, 1851–75* (London, 1971). See especially the section on respectability and gentlemen.

Briggs, Asa, 'The Background of the Parliamentary Reform Movement in Three English Cities', *Cambridge Historical Journal*, X (1950–2).

——, 'Middle-Class Consciousness in English Politics, 1780–1846', *Past and Present*, No. 9 (1956).

——, *The Age of Improvement* (London, 1959(a)). Especially good on the political aspects of class.

——, *Chartist Studies* (London, 1959(b)).

——, 'The Language of "Class" in Early Nineteenth-Century England', in Asa Briggs and John Saville (eds), *Essays in Labour History* (London, 1960); reprinted in M. W. Flinn and T. C. Smout (eds), *Essays in Social History* (Oxford, 1974).

Bythell, D., *The Hand-Loom Weavers: A Study in the English Cotton Industry During the Industrial Revolution* (Cambridge, 1969). Takes careful account of the market position of an important occupational group.

Church, R. A., and Chapman, S. D., 'Gravenor Henson and the Making of the English Working Class', in E. L. Jones and G. E. Mingay (eds), *Land, Labour and Population in the Industrial Revolution* (London, 1967). A criticism of E. P. Thompson (1963).

Clements, R. V., 'British Trades Unions and Popular Political Economy, 1850–1875', *EcHR*, XIV (1961).

Cole, G. D. H., *Attempts at a General Union, 1818–1834* (London, 1953).

Cole, G. D. H., and Postgate, Raymond, *The Common People, 1746–1946* (London, 1938). One of the old Fabian histories.

Crossick, G., 'The Labour Aristocracy and Its Values: A Study of Mid-Victorian Kentish London', *Victorian Studies*, XIV (1976).

Davidoff, Leonore, *The Best Circles: Society, Etiquette and The Season* (London, 1973). A pioneering book, examining the mechanism of status-assertion in the upper class and its relationship to class power.

*Donnelly, F. K., 'Ideology and Early English Working-Class History: Edward Thompson and His Critics', *Social History*, I (1976).

Engels, Frederick, *The Condition of the Working Class in England*

(1845), edited by W. O. Henderson and W. H. Chaloner (Oxford, 1958).

Foster, John, *Class Struggle and the Industrial Revolution: Early Industrial Capitalism in Three English Towns* (London, 1974). See *Social History*, I (1976) for A. E. Musson's criticism and Foster's reply; also John Saville, in *Socialist Register* (1974) and G. Stedman Jones, in *New Left Review* (1975).

Gray, Robert Q., *The Labour Aristocracy in Victorian Edinburgh* (Oxford, 1976). Of wider implication than the title suggests, this is an example of technical excellence in writing about class.

Harrison, B. H., 'Religion and Recreation in Nineteenth-Century England', *Past and Present*, No. 38 (1967).

Harrison, J. F. C., *Learning and Living, 1790–1960* (London, 1961). Early chapters deal with Mechanics Institutions and self-help.

Hay, D., Linebaugh, P., and Thompson, E. P., *Albion's Fatal Tree: Crime and Society in Eighteenth-Century England* (London, 1975). A conflict-view of the society, examining class authority and the legal system.

*Hill, Michael, *A Sociology of Religion* (London, 1973). Chapter 9 is a critical survey of the Halévy thesis on the relationship of Methodism and class.

Hobsbawm, E. J., *The Age of Revolution, 1789–1848* (London, 1962).

——, *Labouring Men: Studies in the History of Labour* (London, 1964) Deals with, among other things, Luddites, Methodism, the tramping artisan, the standard of living, and the labour aristocracy.

Hobsbawm, E. J., and Rudé, G., *Captain Swing* (London, 1969).

Hollis, P., *The Pauper Press* (Oxford, 1970).

*——, *Class and Class-Conflict in Nineteenth-Century England, 1815–1850* (London, 1973).

Hunter, James Robert, *The Making of the Crofting Community* (Edinburgh, 1976). Studies conflict and consciousness in a very different context from most of Britain.

Johnson, Richard, 'Educational Policy and Social Control in Early Victorian England', *Past and Present*, No. 49 (1970).

Kay, James Phillips, *The Moral and Physical Condition of the Working Classes Employed in the Cotton Manufacture in Manchester* (Manchester, 1832; reprinted Didsbury, 1969). A middle-class account of class conflict which should be read along with Engels (1844).

Kemp, B., 'Reflections on the Corn Laws', *Victorian Studies*, V (1961–2).

Kiernan, V., 'Evangelicalism and the French Revolution', *Past and Present*, No. 14 (1952).

Kitson Clark, G., 'The Repeal of the Corn Laws and the Politics of the Forties', *EcHR*, IV (1951–2).

——, 'Hunger and Politics in 1842', *Journal of Modern History*, XXV (1953).

Laslett, P., *The World We Have Lost*, 2nd edn (London, 1971).

McCord, N., *The Anti-Corn Law League, 1838–1846* (London, 1958).

——, 'Cobden and Bright in Politics, 1846–1857', in R. Robson (ed.), *Ideas and Institutions in Victorian Britain* (London, 1967). A critique of the claim these two men made to represent the middle class.

MacLaren, A. A., *Social Class in Scotland, Past and Present* (Edinburgh, 1976). Class is related to housing, disease, sex, thrift and agricultural labour.

Midwinter, E. C., *Law and Order in Early Victorian Lancashire*, Borthwick Paper No. 34 (York, 1968).

*Musson, A. E., *British Trades Unions, 1800–1875* (London, 1972), in the present series.

Neale, R. S., *Class and Ideology in the Nineteenth Century* (London, 1972).

Nossiter, T. J., *Influence, Opinion and Political Idioms in Reformed England: Case Studies from the North East, 1832–74* (Brighton, 1975).

*Pelling, Henry, *A History of British Trade Unionism* (London, 1963; 3rd edn, 1976).

*Perkin, H. J., *The Origins of Modern English Society, 1780–1880* (London, 1969).

Pollard, S., *The Genesis of Modern Management: A Study in the Industrial Revolution* (London, 1965). Examines factory discipline and the organisation of capital.

Prothero, I., 'Chartism in London', *Past and Present*, No. 44 (1969).

Radzinowicz, Leon, *A History of English Criminal Law*, vol. IV (London, 1968). Chapter 4 is the best study of ruling-class attitudes to the crowd.

Read, D., *Peterloo: The Massacre and Its Background* (Manchester, 1958).

Rostow; W. W., *The British Economy of the Nineteenth Century*

(Oxford, 1948). The social tension chart is worth close attention.

Rowe, D. J., 'Class and Political Radicalism in London, 1831 – 32', *Historical Journal*, XIII (1970).

Rudé, G., *The Crowd in History, 1730–1848* (New York, 1964). Deals with the crowd as a social and political phenomenon, and with Luddism and the Plug Riots of 1842.

Saville, John, 'Primitive Accumulation and Early Industrialisation in Britain', *Socialist Register* (1969). Discusses agricultural change in a Marxist context.

Simon, B., *Studies in the History of Education, 1780–1870* (London, 1960). Examines education as a factor in class relationships.

Smout, T. C., *A History of the Scottish People* (London, 1969). Includes, among other things, a study of class north of the border.

Spring, David, 'The English Landed Estate in the Age of Coal and Iron', *Journal of Economic History*, XI (1951).

Stedman Jones, G., *Outcast London: A Study in the Relationships Between Classes in Victorian England* (Oxford, 1971).

Storch, R. D., 'The Plague of Blue Locusts: Police Reform and Popular Resistance in Northern England, 1840–57', *International Review of Social History*, XX (1975).

Thomis, M. I., *The Luddites: Machine-Breaking in Regency England* (Newton Abbott, 1970); and *Politics and Society in Nottingham, 1785–1835* (Oxford, 1963). Both works attack different aspects of E. P. Thompson (1963).

Thompson, D. (ed.), *The Early Chartists* (London, 1971).

Thompson, E. P., *The Making of the English Working Class* (London, 1963). A major study.

——, 'Time, Work Discipline and Industrial Capitalism', *Past and Present*, No. 38 (1967); reprinted in M. W. Flinn and T. C. Smout (eds), *Essays in Social History* (Oxford, 1974).

——, 'The Moral Economy of the English Crowd in the Eighteenth Century', *Past and Present*, No. 50 (1971). Examines grain riots and other disorders.

Thompson, E. P., and Yeo, E., *The Unknown Mayhew* (London, 1971).

Tillotson, Kathleen, *Novels of the Eighteen-Forties* (Oxford, 1954). A valuable study: historians should read more novels.

Turner, H. A., *Trade Union Growth, Structure and Policy* (London, 1962). This begins with a study of the early cotton unions.

Tyrrell, A., 'Class Consciousness in Early Victorian Britain', *Journal of British Studies*, IX (1970). Treats of Samuel Smiles in his radical phase.

Vincent, John, *The Formation of the Liberal Party, 1857—1868* (London, 1966).

——, *Pollbooks: How Victorians Voted* (Cambridge, 1967).

Webb, R. K., *The British Working Class Reader, 1780—1848* (London, 1955).

Webb, S. and B., *The History of Trades Unionism, 1666—1920* (London, 1919). Still useful: see Musson [1972] for revisions.

Western, J. R., 'The Volunteer Movement as an Anti-Revolutionary Force, 1793—1801', *English Historical Review*, LXXI (1956).

Wickham, E. R., *Church and People in an Industrial City* (London, 1957). An experienced industrial chaplain of the 1950s describes attempts made in the nineteenth century to persuade the working class to go to church.

Williams, Gwyn A., *Artisans and Sans Culottes* (London, 1968).

Williams, Raymond, *Culture and Society, 1780—1950* (London, 1958). A survey of the literature of class commentary.

Index

expectations 38, 40, 55

factories 19, 34, 44, 50–51, 52
factory acts 24, 42, 51, 60
fair wages 16, 38
food prices and shortages 38, 40, 47–48
friendly societies 18, 28, 43, 50, 66

Gaskell Mrs, *North and South* 64–65
gentleman 18–19, 65
government growth 25, 63
grain and price riots 16, 18
Gramsci, Antonio 11, 58
Grand National Consolidated Trades Union 28, 50

hegemony 58, 60
Hetherington, Henry 9, 18, 21, 39
homogeniety within classes 13–14, 45

ideals, struggle of 12–14
ideology 16–17, 21–23, 25, 32, 34, 51
immiseration of the proletariat 24
income sources 13, 33
Irish 49, 67

Kay, James P, later James Kay Shuttleworth 9, 21, 59, 69
keelmen 17

labour aristocracy 25
labour consciousness 37, 40
labour market 14, 23, 47, 51, 53, 62
land market 15, 34
landlords and landowners 13–14, 23, 32
landowners and status 64
Leeds 34, 42, 65
Leeds woollen merchants 17
legal system 13, 21, 38

legitimate power 19, 39, 40
opposition to 16
leisure 53, 58
London 16–17, 34, 55, 57, 65
Luddites 20, 30, 39, 44, 45, 48, 52

magistrates 14, 15, 17, 38, 40
manchester 9–10, 50, 52
manufacturers 10, 13, 15, 19, 57, 64–65
of cotton 52
marriage 27, 29, 33, 34, 65
Marx, Karl 10–11, 21–26
Mayhew, Henry 34, 56
Mechanics Institutions 59, 60
merchants 16–18
Methodism 39, 67
middle class 9, 13, 22, 28–29, 32–34, 44, 52, 59–60, 64, 66, 67
and interest groups 37
middle ranks 19
miners 17, 18, 44
mob, the 18, 19

Napier, General Sir Charles James 57
nationalism 67
Newcastle 1740 riot 17
North–East England 17, 18, 34
novels 64–65

Oldham 33, 35–36, 39–44, 52
Owenism and the Owenites 39, 41, 55

Paine, Thomas 19, 20, 30, 35, 37–39, 45, 48, 68
Paley, Archdeacon 9, 15
paternalism 9, 12–14, 52–53
patronage 19
peasants 22, 32, 49
people the, 18–19, 39
Perkin, H J, *The Origins of Modern English Society* 12
Peterloo 30, 39, 54, 68
petty bourgeoisie 33, 62